A Student's Guide to the MA TESOL

A Student's Guide to the MA TESOL

Nancy Bell
Washington State University, USA

First published 2009 by
PALGRAVE MACMILLAN

Palgrave Macmillan in the UK is an imprint of Macmillan Publishers Limited,
registered in England, company number 785998, of Houndmills, Basingstoke,
Hampshire RG21 6XS.

Palgrave Macmillan in the US is a division of St Martin's Press LLC,
175 Fifth Avenue, New York, NY 10010.

Palgrave Macmillan is the global academic imprint of the above companies
and has companies and representatives throughout the world.

Palgrave® and Macmillan® are registered trademarks in the United States,
the United Kingdom, Europe and other countries.

ISBN-13: 978–0–230–22430–8 hardback
ISBN-13: 978–0–230–22431–5 paperback

This book is printed on paper suitable for recycling and made from fully
managed and sustained forest sources. Logging, pulping and manufacturing
processes are expected to conform to the environmental regulations of the
country of origin.

A catalogue record for this book is available from the British Library.

A catalog record for this book is available from the Library of Congress.

10   9   8   7   6   5   4   3   2   1
18   17   16   15   14   13   12   11   10   09

Printed and bound in Great Britain by
CPI Antony Rowe, Chippenham and Eastbourne

Contents

Preface

I never planned to be a teacher. In fact, the idea never even crossed my mind giving me the opportunity to dismiss it. Always an avid reader, I came to college as an undergraduate assuming that I would study English literature, but I fell into linguistics after reading some course descriptions in the university catalog. Although it did not turn out to involve four years of anagrams and other word games as I had somehow envisioned, each step of the way I was fascinated. When we studied morphology, I wanted to be a morphologist. While taking sociolinguistics, I wanted to be a sociolinguist. During my syntax course, I wanted to . . . well, that one didn't follow the usual pattern. Still, had my final coursework been in phonology, I might instead be writing right now about sound patterns in the west African language Mafa. Instead, as it turned out, the last classes I took were in second language acquisition and second language teaching methods.

On the advice of my undergraduate mentor, I applied to work with the US Peace Corps, with little understanding of what that meant. They kept sending me paperwork, I kept filling it out, and eventually they sent me a plane ticket – so I went. After two years of teaching English in Cameroon, I returned to the US and happened upon a private language school, which allowed me to continue to work as an ESL instructor, despite having only a BA degree. Although a friend laughed hysterically when one of my students described me as 'so patient,' I had discovered, to my own surprise, that I loved teaching. Obtaining an MA in TESOL (Teaching English to Speakers of Other Languages) was a natural next step to bolster my knowledge and credentials for job security and advancement.

That, too, is a story of blind faith and dumb luck, and given my naiveté, I feel lucky to be teaching today. The upshot of all this, however, is that, despite my initial blundering, thanks to numerous friends, colleagues, and professors who were kind, generous, and patient about sharing advice, I learned a great deal along the way. I hope to pass on some of the wisdom I gleaned from others, as well as from my own mistakes, in hopes of smoothing your path through graduate school.

I know from experience that students beginning a graduate program often do so with a great deal of trepidation, and if they do not feel this before the first day of class, they often do after meeting classmates who seem well informed and articulate, or after receiving a detailed syllabus outlining hundreds of pages of reading and writing to be completed during the semester. Although students normally go to graduate school in order to expand their knowledge, the amount of learning to be done can be daunting. Students who have some background in ESL theory or methods, or who have experience teaching, may suddenly feel like they know very little.

In addition, an MA program assumes specialization in some area, and with this comes specialized ways of speaking and writing. TESOL is no different, but despite our focus on language learning, professors' expectations regarding these skills are not often expressed overtly for new students, who must learn implicitly through participating in class and through trial and error.

The goal of this book is to discuss clearly and openly many of the assumptions and controversies in the field of TESOL in order to help new MA TESOL students begin their graduate programs with confidence and finish successfully. The aim is not to provide complete summaries of, or definitive answers to, questions about such topics as teaching methodology and second language acquisition, as there are numerous texts that provide excellent overviews: many of these are cited in this book, and I have tried to err on the side of more recent, rather than classic citations, as you will find classic work cited in these newer publications as well. Rather, it is my hope that this book can help guide your expectations for an MA TESOL program and serve as a resource for success within that program.

The text is organized in two parts. Part I introduces the field of TESOL, providing an overview of important concepts and controversies within the discipline. As you read, you will consider what teaching and learning mean, what the role of theory is for TESOL instructors, and what issues you may face when deciding which variety of English to teach. In addition, a discussion of current views of how to teach will hopefully dispel any expectations that your program will provide you with an arsenal of sure-fire techniques or recipes that you can follow to ensure that your students learn English successfully. Chapter 1 introduces the field and provides some historical background, while Chapter 2 discusses theories related to three important components of TESOL: language, teaching, and learning. The final chapter in Part I introduces a number of concepts in TESOL that are important influences on second language teaching and learning, and of current interest in the field. This first part may not *answer* your questions, but it should guide you toward an understanding of the kinds of questions you should expect to consider, in your graduate program and in your own future classroom.

Part II provides some relief for those who picked up this text seeking practical, down-to-earth advice. Chapter 4 discusses the experience of learning to 'do' graduate school; that is, it explores the process of socialization into the TESOL community during graduate school. Here you will learn more about activities and expectations you are likely to encounter during your MA program. Chapter 5 addresses ways to find and understand research in order to become a better-informed ESL teacher and to write stronger course papers. Finally, although it may seem too early to be thinking about returning to the world of work, preparation for the job market during graduate school can make it much easier to obtain a first job, therefore the final chapter contains suggestions for strengthening your professional qualifications now.

The main audience for this book is new MA TESOL students and it can be used in a variety of ways. It might be read prior to starting a program as a way of preparing students for the concepts they will encounter, or it could be used as a text in the first course students take in their new program. Professors who opt to use this as an introductory text will certainly want to supplement it with their favorite readings in each area, or assign the suggested readings that accompany each chapter in order to examine specific topics in greater detail. For example, the three main sections of Chapter 2, language, learning, and teaching, might be spread over several different classes with supplementary readings assigned for each section. In addition, it is likely that professors will want to present the information in different order. For instance, Chapter 5, which discusses research, may be presented fairly early in a course as a way of helping students begin work on assigned projects.

Finally, note that as with any new group that you become involved in, applied linguists and second language instructors have specialized language that must be learned. Words in bold can be found in the glossary at the end of this text. Acronyms also abound, and before you begin reading, you may want to take note of some of the more common one. A fuller list can be found in Appendix A, but these are a few to get you started:

ELT	English language teaching
ESL	English as a second* language
L1	first, or native language
L2	second* language
NS, NNS	native speaker, non-native speaker
SLA	second* language acquisition

* Note that 'second' here does not refer merely to the order in which a language was learned, but is generally used in the sense of 'additional,' to include all languages learned after the mother tongue.

Acknowledgements

This book would not have come to fruition without my graduate students, who trusted me enough to express their professional questions and anxieties candidly, and in doing so made me a better teacher. I would also like to express my gratitude to the following colleagues who shared ideas and feedback on early drafts, and whose suggestions greatly improved the final product: Sharon Deckert, Carolin Fuchs, Sarah Gordon, Nancy Hayward, Anne Pomerantz, Keith Richards, and Victor Villanueva.

My parents, Rodland and Celene Bell, also deserve special appreciation for providing a careful, non-specialist reading – their persistent pleas for clearer, simpler language and explanations contributed a great deal to the readability of the text.

And, as always, many thanks to Mark.

Part I

An Introduction to the Discipline of TESOL

1
Situating Ourselves

Who are we? What exactly does this field encompass? The truth is that while any TESOL program will be devoted to helping you learn the theory and pedagogy of English language education, they can reflect a wide variety of perspectives, thus it is important to begin by situating ourselves. We will look at our location from a broad perspective when I offer an abbreviated history of TESOL as a way of understanding its interdisciplinary roots and current location. You will also have an opportunity to consider where your own MA program is situated within the university structure and how this might affect your education. TESOL programs housed in departments of English, Education, and Applied Linguistics can differ widely in the courses they offer and the perspectives they privilege. We will close by situating ourselves with respect to terminology, and discuss the ways that it can vary within the field. Let's begin, however, at the micro level, by examining who we are as individuals within a group of professionals, and by thinking about your own reasons for obtaining this degree and about the different kinds of people you might meet in your program.

Locating yourself

TESOL programs attract students from overseas, as well as those from the local area where the program is offered. People from each group may be obtaining the degree in order to teach in a variety of contexts within their home country, such as state schools, private language schools, universities, and primary or secondary institutions. Others

3

may see an MA TESOL as a way to travel, obtaining teaching positions around the world. Some students may be starting the program directly after completing an undergraduate degree, whereas others may have been working in a completely different field for years and are looking to change careers. Sometimes even highly experienced ESL instructors seek an MA TESOL while taking leave from their current position in order to bolster their credentials or simply as a way of refreshing themselves. With such a variety of individuals, you can often learn at least as much from your colleagues in the program as you can from the actual coursework.

The questions below (and throughout this text) are best done in groups with fellow students, but they are worthwhile to consider even if you are reading this in solitude before the start of your program, as they will help you define your goals and expectations, giving you a baseline from which to judge the ways in which they change:

- Why have you chosen to get an advanced degree in TESOL?
- Why did you choose this particular graduate program for your degree?
- What do you expect and hope to learn in your graduate program? Did these hopes and expectations come from prior teaching and learning experiences? From reading program materials? From talking to other ESL instructors? From talking to students and professors in this program?
- If you are discussing these questions in a group, can you identify any qualities that seem to be characteristic of ESL instructors?

Of course, with any group there is wide variation in individual characteristics, but at the same time, people who come together for any specific purpose do tend to share traits. As a whole, I find that those of us with an interest in teaching ESL tend to enjoy language – using it, playing with it, comparing it to other languages. TESOL practitioners are also usually enthusiastic about seeking out intercultural experiences. Many have a strong sense of social justice and a desire to improve the human condition. The teaching, for some, comes as a natural (or accidental, as I have already confessed) outgrowth of these interests. Sometimes, however, the desire to teach comes first, and it is only after encountering non-native English speakers in their classes that the interest in finding out more about language and intercultural communication grows. In any case, what all those who seek an MA TESOL have in common with regard to teaching is the desire to learn to do it better.

Along with your developing sense of where you fit into the field, there is also the question of how TESOL itself is situated with respect to other academic areas. As I have mentioned, this is an interdisciplinary field and you may initially feel a bit at sea and find it difficult to see how all the strands fit together. While you will eventually sort this out, it won't happen right away (in fact, it may not happen until after you have graduated!), but a short history might help you begin to make sense of where TESOL comes from, why it looks as it does today, and where it fits in the larger academic scheme.

Locating the roots of TESOL

Histories are always written for a purpose, and as such are selective in the information they present according to that purpose. This one is no different. Numerous excellent and very thorough histories of the field of second language (L2) education exist and you will doubtless encounter some of them in your studies (e.g., Musumeci, 1997; Richards and Rodgers, 2001; Howatt and Widdowson, 2004). My goal in this section is only to provide you with a sense of the interdisciplinary roots of the field in order to prepare you for the wide range of information you will encounter in your graduate studies. As such, I have skipped over thousands of years of history and commenced our story at the moment in time just before the emergence of the field of applied linguistics, of which TESOL makes up an important part. I also focus on traditions in North America and Europe, which have dominated the field; however, it is important to note that a variety of international perspectives exist and while these have, in the past, received very little attention from Western scholars, their value is increasingly recognized and efforts are being made to increase awareness and dissemination of this work (Canagarajah, 2002; for an overview of emerging trends in applied linguistics globally, see Gass and Makoni, 2004).

In Europe and the US, prior to the late 1800s, language was largely taught similarly to other subjects, such as history or mathematics. Teachers used the students' native language to present vocabulary and grammatical rules about the **target language**, and this was followed by translation exercises. The result was that students learned *about* language rather than learning to *use* language, rather like a mechanic who can explain in detail the workings of a combustion engine, but who has never learned to drive. This way of teaching was known as the Grammar-Translation Method and, as Richards and Rodgers (2001) describe it, '[i]t is a method for which there is no theory. There is no literature that offers a rationale or justification for it or that attempts to relate it to issues in linguistics, psychology, or educational theory' (p. 7). This comfortable state of atheoretical affairs may have continued if it were not for two important developments. First, the technological breakthroughs of the industrial revolution made communication among and travel in European countries much easier, and learners began to clamor for oral proficiency in foreign languages. Also around this time the field of linguistics was undergoing a major shift and turning its focus to phonetics, and with these changes the Grammar-Translation Method began to give way to a theorized approach.

Phonetics is the branch of linguistics that seeks to describe the physical properties of sounds of language. You may already know the International Phonetic Alphabet, which provides a common set of symbols for speech sounds, the first version of which was created in 1888. This new interest in cataloging the sounds of the world's languages had the effect of focusing attention on speech, rather than reading, as had previously been the case. As linguists weighed in on the issue of how best to teach language, instructors were encouraged to provide linguistic input orally before doing so in writing, to privilege pronunciation over grammar, and to use mainly the target language, avoiding translation. One approach, known as the Direct Method, grew in part out of these recommendations. You may be familiar with a well-known version of this approach still popular today: the Berlitz Method.

This emphasis on oral language continued when structuralism became the dominant linguistic paradigm from about the 1930s, and shifted the focus to language as a complex, but ordered system. The movement is generally recognized as beginning with **Ferdinand de Saussure**'s 1906–11 lectures, which were later developed by other scholars, perhaps most prominently **Roman Jakobson** of the Prague School of linguistics. He and other structural linguists turned their attention to the systematic collection and analysis of language samples, with the goal of exhaustively describing their **phonological, morphological,** and **syntactic** rules. This alone may not have caused great changes in language education, but when joined with concurrent developments in psychology, where **behaviorism** became the dominant paradigm, a vast shift can be seen in the field.

Behaviorists saw human learning as a habitual response to stimuli. The well-known behavioral psychologist **B. F. Skinner** (1957) saw language learning, too, as the result of repeated exposure to sounds (words, sentences) and the reinforcement or change to the learner's behavior that occurred following their response. Thus, it was thought that a child who said, 'Yesterday I visit my friend' would receive negative reinforcement in the form of a correction, and therefore learn to say 'visited' when referring to the past. In the 1950s, particularly in the US, the result of the union of behavioral psychology and structural linguistics was an early account of language learning that was also used to create a specific teaching methodology, audiolingualism. In this approach teachers used pattern drills and repeated performances of memorized dialogues to develop their students' linguistic 'habits.' The instructor carefully monitored these for errors, which received immediate correction to prevent the internalization of improper language habits.

Robert Lado (1957) further developed these views with respect to L2 learning, proposing that differences between the first language (L1) and target language were the cause of errors in L2 learning. At this point we can clearly see that a new field, applied linguistics, has emerged, and subsequent developments in language education are driven by theory and research. Lado believed that careful analysis and comparison of the structures of the first and second languages, known as contrastive analysis, would allow predictions to be made concerning when differences might facilitate learning and when they might give rise to error. This would then help teachers using the audiolingual method to present materials in an orderly manner and to provide the negative reinforcement necessary to eliminate errors.

Yet, despite this careful surveillance, teachers soon found that errors persisted. Researchers, too, encountered challenges, as they began to find that contrastive analysis did not accurately predict which structures would be easy or difficult to learn. But perhaps most damaging to the behaviorist view of language acquisition were linguist **Noam Chomsky's** (1959) critiques, which showed that it was far from able to provide a comprehensive account of the language learning process. Not only do parents only rarely correct their children's grammar, but children (as well as L2 learners) are able to use and understand creative and unique language far beyond what they have been exposed to. Applied linguist **S. Pit Corder** (1967) advanced this view further, reconceptualizing error as a normal part of L2 development. Researchers began to look closely at **'interlanguage,'** a term coined by **Larry Selinker** (1972) to describe the evolving state of the learner's L2 knowledge. Numerous studies in the 1970s traced the acquisition of morphemes and syntactic structures in L1 (e.g., Brown, 1973; de Villiers and de Villiers, 1973) and L2 acquisition (Dulay and Burt, 1973, 1974; Bailey, Madden, and Krashen, 1974; Larsen-Freeman, 1976), finding that they followed virtually the same developmental path across L1 learners, as well as child and adult L2 learners.

At the same time, sociolinguist and anthropologist **Dell Hymes** demonstrated a shortcoming in the Chomskyian approach to language. Chomsky (1965) viewed linguistic competence as the underlying grammatical knowledge of a hypothetical, ideal native speaker-hearer. That is, his interest was in the knowledge of language itself, and language use, with its slips of the tongue, incomplete sentences, and stuttering was clearly not representative of a speaker's competence. Hymes (1972a, 1972b), on the other hand, drew attention to language use and the important role that culture plays in it, showing that in order to communicate effectively a speaker needs to be able not only to form grammatically correct sentences, but to apply them in conjunction with rules of use. In other words, the speaker must know how, when, where, and with whom to use various linguistic forms. Consider, for example, the following two possible requests:

1. Give me juice.
2. I juice, please?

The L1 or L2 learner who attempts to request a glass of juice using the second, grammatically incorrect, but polite formulation may receive a more sympathetic response than the learner whose response is grammatical, as in the first example, but probably seen as rude.

Although Hymes was originally directing his work at language issues surrounding disadvantaged children, his notions were quickly taken up by researchers in the field of second language acquisition (SLA), who began to focus on helping L2 learners develop **communicative competence** (Hymes, 1972b; see also Canale and Swain, 1980).

While Hymes' views were prevalent in the US, European and Australian scholars were also critiquing Chomsky's view of competence in somewhat different ways. An enormously influential perspective that gained ground during this time is **M. A. K. Halliday's** Systemic Functional Linguistics (SFL). Unlike Chomsky's approach to language, which placed linguistic forms as primary, Halliday (1973, 1975) saw form and function as inseparable, with both arising out of the need to construct meaning in interaction with others. Social context is also important, as different language-using situations call for the use of different linguistic resources to create meanings particular to that context. Certain features of language tend to occur together regularly in a specific context, resulting in a fairly predictable set of choices for any given situation. For children, complex, extended interaction with caregivers exposes them to a variety of meanings and the ways that language patterns to create these meanings, resulting in their simultaneously learning *through* and *about* language (see also Painter, 1999). L2 scholars saw applications for ESL instruction in Halliday's ideas, and out of this developed programs that focused on teaching the language that is typically used in a given situation, known as teaching **English for Specific Purposes** (ESP). Thus, while similar in its embrace of language use in context, the SFL model moved beyond the level of words and sentences, to teach **genres** of language use, a practice that continues to grow in influence today. (See Chapter 4 for a discussion of genres you are likely to encounter in your graduate program.)

During the 1970s, influenced by the theories of Hymes and Halliday, language teachers and researchers came to recognize that acquiring a language requires much more than the internalization of its structure and vocabulary. Accordingly, the L2 classroom began to focus more on functions, meaning, and communication within specific situations, rather than solely on linguistic forms. Also, because the morpheme order studies seemed to be showing that the order in which linguistic structures were acquired was both fixed and natural, error correction was considered less or not at all useful. Learners spent more time in the classroom in open discussion, with errors rarely corrected by the teacher. Memorization gave way to creative language use, and communication and fluency came to be valued over grammatical accuracy. Due to the influence of Hymes and other sociolinguists, more attention began to be paid to cultural variation in social patterns and rules of use and how these could be seen as a potential contributor to cross-linguistic misunderstandings. The innovations that grew from Halliday's work involved analysis of language-using situations to identify and describe the typical (or generic) linguistic features that occurred in oral or written texts and sought to raise learner awareness of them. Michael Swan refers to this as both a 'bewildering' and 'exhilarating' time in the profession, as new theories and methods proliferated, prompting many teachers to choose an eclectic mix of approaches (Brown et al., 2006, p. 4). It was at this time, too, that a method that remains highly influential today, Communicative Language Teaching, with its emphasis on language *use* (rather than *form*), got its start.

Although its roots lie earlier, Communicative Language Teaching gained support in the 1980s through **Stephen Krashen**'s (1981, 1985) highly influential Monitor Model. This theory of SLA proposed that learning occurred naturally from exposure to 'comprehensible input,' that is, language that was just slightly above the learner's current stage of interlanguage development, described as 'i + 1.' Krashen also distinguished acquisition from learning. The former was seen as an unconscious process by which learners create utterances. Fluent L2 use, in this view, came through acquisition, whereas learned language, which developed through a conscious process, was seen as useful only for monitoring output, and even then, only under optimal conditions when learners have the time, linguistic knowledge, and desire to check the form of their utterances. Acquisition, too, might be hindered if a learner were bored or anxious, which would cause the psychological barrier that Krashen referred to as the 'affective filter' to be raised, thus blocking input.

Language teachers found the Monitor Model intuitively appealing and appreciated its immediate classroom implications. For example, given the importance of acquisition over learning, and the restricted conditions under which the monitor could operate, instructors could avoid explicit instruction on grammar and instead focus on providing contexts for learners to obtain comprehensible **input**. In addition, the idea of the affective filter suggested that a nurturing, rather than punitive, classroom environment would benefit L2 development. Thus, group discussions and problem-solving activities became important components of Communicative Language Teaching. In these formats learners could work together in a relaxed manner, with a focus on language content rather than form. Despite this enthusiasm, Krashen's work was subjected to vigorous criticisms by SLA researchers (for some well-known examples, see Sharwood Smith, 1981; Gregg, 1984; McLaughlin, 1987). While the Monitor Model is no longer considered a viable description of SLA, this work was highly influential and forced the field to clarify its research agenda.

Specifically, Krashen's input hypothesis spurred interest in discerning the exact nature of the relationship between interaction and language learning. Research in this area grew throughout the 1980s and 1990s, and continues at present. One way of exploring this was through the use of information gap **tasks**, which focused learners' attention on meaning and made an exchange of information a requirement for successful completion of the task. For example, two learners might be given two different weekly schedules and be asked to try to find a time for both to meet, without showing each other their schedules (see Chapter 2 for more discussion of language learning tasks). By observing and analyzing their interaction, SLA researchers came to see the importance of the act of negotiating meaning for language learning.

Initially, the nature of the input learners received from native speakers (NSs) was the focus of this research (Hatch, 1983; Long, 1983; Gass and Varonis, 1985), but now the impact of **negotiation** and interactional adjustments (Pica, 1994; Mackey, 1999), learner output (Swain, 1985; Izumi and Izumi, 2004), and feedback (Philp, 2003; Mackey and Goo, 2007) have all been all closely investigated. This work has become the basis for what is known as the Interaction Hypothesis, which, while not yet a complete explanation of SLA (hence the use of 'hypothesis' rather than 'theory'), the model, discussed in more detail in Chapter 2, currently provides one of the most compelling perspectives.

The tasks used in these research projects have also come into wide pedagogical use, marking the first revolutionary change in teaching since communicative language teaching moved the priority from grammatical accuracy, to meaning and fluency. Explicit attention to form has again become important, as grammatical errors were found to persist when learners focused solely on communicating meaning (Swain, 1985). Now, however, instead of pattern drills, carefully designed tasks help teachers maintain a focus on meaning, while also drawing learners' attention to L2 forms (for discussions of task-based language teaching, see R. Ellis, 2000, 2003; van den Branden, 2006). Understanding how and when to emphasize form and meaning in the classroom remains an important area of concern for teachers and researchers.

By the 1990s, a good number of applied linguists, in a movement that included scholars from many academic disciplines, had begun to investigate the significance for applied linguistics of the social theories of post-modern, post-structural, and post-colonial scholars such as feminist philosophers Judith Butler and Julia Kristeva, sociologist Pierre Bourdieu, and literary and political critic Edward Said. This led to a new focus, for some, on the sociopolitical context of language learning. Rather than looking at negotiation as a *neutral* matter of linguistic adjustments, new research highlighted the socially constructed nature of interaction, and the ways in which power and identity affected approaches and outcomes to language learning (e.g., Bremer et al., 1996; Siegal, 1996; Ibrahim, 1999; Norton, 2000). Many of these studies showed how learners were often treated unequally in conversation, and how this marginalization negatively impacted on their language acquisition. Others sought to explore unsatisfactory learning outcomes as part of student resistance to educational practices that did not meet their needs or were alienating. Thus, we also turned a critical eye toward our own profession to examine the ways in which English language teaching (ELT) may contribute to colonialism and oppression (Phillipson, 1992; Canagarajah, 1999).

Exploration of these new perspectives (many of which, it should be noted, had long been in use by other disciplines) led to new descriptions and theories of SLA. This abundance of theories and approaches to the study of SLA has, in a series of debates, been both lauded as a sign of a healthy and growing field (van Lier, 1994; Block, 1996; Lantolf, 1996, 2002; Firth and Wagner, 1997, 1998), and decried as indicative of an unscientific approach or a lack of focus (Gregg, 1993, 2000; Beretta et al., 1994; Gregg et al., 1997; Long, 1997, 1998; Gass,

1998). Much of the debate involves the goals of research in SLA and the relative importance of cognitive versus social perspectives on language and language learning.

At present, several viable theories exist, some in competition with others to explain (part of) how L2 development takes place, while others tend to be more complementary. While the debates continue (see, e.g., the December 2007 issue of the *Modern Language Journal*, which revisited the impact of Firth and Wagner, 1997, the article which touched off much of the lively discussion mentioned above), many in the field have recognized the value and necessity of both cognitive and social perspectives to explain SLA and have been pursuing promising avenues of inquiry that attempt to unite these views. Merrill Swain and her colleague Sharon Lapkin (Swain, 2000, 2006; Swain and Lapkin, 2002, 2006) for example, have been integrating the interactionist perspective with sociocultural theory. Scholars such as Claire Kramsch (2002, Kramsch and Whiteside, 2008) and Leo van Lier (2004) have emphasized an ecological perspective to SLA. From the world of mathematics, led by Diane Larsen-Freeman (Larsen-Freeman, 1997; Larsen-Freeman and Cameron, 2008; see also de Bot, 2008; de Bot, Lowie, and Verspoor, 2007), complexity or dynamic systems theory has also challenged those in our field to rethink their views of language learning and teaching, along with a related perspective, emergentism (N. Ellis, 1998; see also the 2006 *Applied Linguistics* special issue).

As I cautioned at the beginning of this section, this is a very simplified version of the history of SLA and ELT, designed to introduce you to the multiple academic perspectives that you are likely to encounter in your studies. It may seem that our field is composed of dichotomies – form vs. meaning, accuracy vs. fluency, cognitive vs. social – and indeed, the changes have often been portrayed using a pendulum as a metaphor, with TESOL professionals swinging wildly between two fixed points. Yet, this metaphor is inadequate, as it is unable to represent the progress that takes place. Mitchell and Vidal (2001) suggest instead using a metaphor of flowing water, with main streams and smaller tributaries that join or split off from these. This allows us to conceptualize progress, as well as to trace the ebb and flow of ideas, many of which are presented as new, although their source is in the distant past.

Given the diversity of language learners and learning contexts we likely need to acknowledge the improbability of any single theory ever sufficing to explain all aspects of language acquisition. For MA TESOL students this can be bewildering and sometimes frustrating: How can we know how to teach if we do not know how people learn? Or indeed, what language itself is, and thus what needs to be taught? It has become clear that no single method will ever be able to claim it is 'the best.' Indeed, we are now firmly in the 'post-method' era (Kumaravadivelu, 1994, 2001), where teachers construct their lessons using flexible principles, rather than rigid methods and procedures. As Dick Allwright (2006) has described it, rather than trying to alter our methods for each individual learner, we can 'acknowledge that this is asking far too much and decide instead to adopt a "scattergun" approach, whereby you offer a multitude of learning opportunities for learners, and expect them to select according to their own particular needs' (p. 14). (Readers who are gun-shy may prefer the more pacifist gardening metaphor which he also provides, in which rather than planting seeds one by one, they are spread more thickly, but haphazardly, under the assumption that some at least will fall where conditions will be conducive to growth).

As you can see, then, your MA program is not going to provide you with a fixed set of practices for teaching ESL – there is no definitive recipe book to follow or bag of tricks from which to choose. So what, then, will you learn? As with so many other questions in TESOL, the answer, as you'll see below is, 'It depends.'

Locating MA programs: what will *you* study?

Of course, you will study how people learn and teach a second language, but what does that include? As you saw in the brief history presented above, TESOL is influenced by many disciplines, but primarily applied linguistics and education. These, too, are influenced by psychology, sociology, and anthropology. Some studies in TESOL follow a traditional scientific paradigm, for example proposing hypotheses about learning and dividing students into treatment and control groups to test the hypotheses (e.g. Pica et al., 1996; Morgan-Short and Bowden, 2006). Others involve qualitative studies in which interviewing and observation are important methods, and small numbers of participants share their experiences in great detail (e.g. Lin, 1999; Harklau, 2000). Still others rely on technology to conduct experiments that tell us more about how an L2 is processed by examining, for example, brain response to violations of grammatical rules (e.g. Tokowicz and MacWhinney, 2005) or eye movement during L2 reading (e.g. Frenck-Mestre and Pynte, 1997). Some combine research methods (e.g. Foster and Ohta, 2006). Thus, you can expect to read a wide variety of research accounts in your program, from those that feel more like narratives, to those that report their findings largely through statistics.

You are also likely to study more theory than you might have expected. Many new instructors want to know the nuts and bolts of *how* to teach (and who can blame them?) and see discussions of theory (that is, *why* to teach a particular way) as only indirectly related to their teaching. Yet, as Henry Widdowson points out, '[t]eachers who insist that they are simply practitioners, workers at the chalkface, not interested in theory, in effect conspire against their own authority, and against their own profession' (2003, p. 2). That is, by upholding the view that teaching is simply 'common sense' (another concept roundly criticized by Widdowson), we suggest that anyone with a good knowledge of English can join the profession. Yet we know that this is not the case. Teachers gain specialized knowledge through observing and reflecting upon their own and others' teaching, questioning not only how, but why certain practices are employed, and 'to reflect on practice in this way,' Widdowson maintains, 'is to theorize about it' (p. 3).

Experience certainly counts for a great deal in the classroom, but as Amy Tsui (2003) reminds us, it is not to be confused with expertise. In other words, time spent in the classroom does not automatically produce an expert teacher; development is ongoing as instructors continually face new challenges in the classroom, and a cycle of reflection and action – in other words, theorizing – is critical. Familiarity with a wide variety of theories of teaching and language learning provides teachers with a stronger base from which to assess and critique new ideas, as well as to develop their own theories. In a recent discussion in *TESOL Quarterly* on the role of theory in the field, Diane Larsen-Freeman (2008) reiterated the recursive relationship between theory and practical experience, adding that theory also works to 'make the unconscious conscious,' allowing us 'to see and name things that might otherwise have escaped our attention' (p. 292).

In teacher education we have been moving away from the positivist scientific paradigm, which assumes that there are (single, true, unbiased) answers to research questions. When this view was in place, teacher education was a matter of 'feeding' future instructors information about their subject matter and the best methods for passing that subject matter on to their students. Now however, we recognize that there can be no single, universal truth and that the choices teachers make are situated – that is, they are grounded in the context in which that teacher works, and informed not only by the current students, administration, and curriculum, but by a multitude of other factors, including the physical surroundings, and historical, social, cultural, political, and economic conditions (Auerbach, 1995; Chick, 1996).

What does all of this mean for you, as an ESL teacher? You will probably find that your program will encourage you to examine your own beliefs and practices with an eye toward developing the ability to critically examine and reflect upon your teaching situation in order to construct the best possible learning environment. Engaging with theory can be an exciting part of this process, as Tim McNamara recalls in describing what theory did for him when he began an MA program after six years of teaching:

> I found that theory broke up a lot of old concrete in my head. It challenged most of my cherished beliefs about language teaching and learning and as a result made the classroom a much more interesting place.
>
> (2008, p. 302)

The value of teachers' knowledge is now recognized, and it is currently the norm to view teacher education more as a kind of apprenticeship, with instructors learning about educational theory and practices, and evaluating and interpreting them in light of their own experiences (both as students and teachers) and the particularities of their educational context. This also opens the possibility for you to participate in helping to explore and answer some of the many questions that remain in our field. (This will be discussed again in Chapter 5, where the role of research for ESL instructors is examined.)

I can nearly guarantee that you will encounter a similar landscape in any MA TESOL program, which will include discussions of theories of language teaching and learning, techniques for teaching language, and activities for continuing professional development. However, each program will view this same terrain from a particular perspective, emphasizing certain aspects of the discipline more than others. This was best illustrated by Vai Ramanathan, Catherine Davies, and Mary Schleppegrell (2001), who compared the MA TESOL programs of two universities in the US, one housed within a department of linguistics, the other in an English department. As might be expected, students in the former program took a number of courses focusing on linguistics (**phonetics, semantics, syntax**), whereas the latter program had a greater focus on L2 literacy, and students there took coursework in teaching L2 writing and using literature in the ESL composition classroom. The programs also had differences that were related to concerns particular to the states where they were located, for example, the west coast university was more attuned to immigration and bilingual education issues. The authors note that while the graduates of both programs exit with a solid grounding in L2 theory and pedagogy, their specific types of expertise are quite different.

Knowledge is often thought to be neutral and free from value judgments, yet this study shows how it is instead intimately tied to ideologies and politics. An example, discussed in greater detail in Chapter 5, is the way that understandings of classroom interactions produced by researchers has tended to be valued more than such knowledge when produced by the ESL teachers themselves. Beliefs about the roles of teachers and students in the learning process, about the nature of language, and even about knowledge itself influence what ideas are presented in an MA program and how. It is important to recognize from the outset that your education will be partial and will be colored by the particular conditions of the context in which it is situated. The agendas of specific professors, of the department, of the university, and of the wider society will all influence what is discussed in the classroom, how it is discussed, and what is excluded. The same, of course, is true for classrooms around the world, and you can use this as an opportunity to step back and take note of how knowledge gets shaped in order to prepare you to take up this same issue in your own classroom.

Locating language: terminology in TESOL

While in graduate school I started taking pottery classes, and although it was quite some time before I created a usable mug, the effect on my vocabulary was immediate. 'Wedge' became a verb describing a way of getting air out of clay, a 'rib' was a tool for shaping pots, and 'cone 10' was a very hot temperature. Whenever you become part of a new group, you need to learn new language and TESOL is no different. As you can see from the examples at the beginning of this chapter of the types of people who study ELT and their reasons for undertaking this degree, the acronym 'TESOL' represents a range of professional possibilities. As an interdisciplinary field, you will find your language learning task complicated a bit by the fact that different people use different terms for similar phenomena or that the same term is used differently by various people.

One of the most immediate places where this becomes obvious is in the manner in which English language teaching, learning and students are referred to in various contexts. In the US and Australia, ESL (English as a second language) has been the most common acronym employed for general purposes. Although this term seems to refer strictly to a specific learning order, it has generally been understood as encompassing a range of learning conditions, including the learning of English as a third or fourth language, for example. In the UK, this imprecision has been reduced by the use of the acronym EAL (English as an additional language). There is also no agreement on the name of the profession itself. In the US, TESOL (teaching English to speakers of other languages) or TESL (teaching English as a second language) tend to be the broadest references, whereas in the UK ELT (English language teaching) predominates.

Another traditional distinction has been between ESL and EFL (English as a foreign language). The former is meant to refer to situations where English is being learned in a country in which it is the dominant language, such as New Zealand or England, whereas the latter refers to contexts like Japan, where English is not a primary local language, and is thus likely to be learned and used mainly within a classroom. Although the acronyms ESL and EFL are still in use, changes like globalization and the development of the internet have blurred the distinction, as these terms misleadingly tie languages to nationalities, ignoring the complex realities of language choice and use among different populations within and across national boundaries (Nayar, 1997; Pennycook, 2003). These same changes have also led to the use of terms like EIL (English as an international language) and ELF (English as a lingua franca) to refer to the teaching of varieties of English that are used, often between non-native speakers (NNSs), for wider communication. Although I will not tease out the differences here, it is worth noting that the use of these terms, as well as others I have not mentioned, differ within each country according to the level of school. The vocabulary used by English language teachers in primary and secondary schools differs from that used by those who teach adults in higher education or immigrant education settings. Fortunately, there is enough overlap to make these distinctions comprehensible, and you will quickly become familiar with those that are in the greatest use in your context.

These acronyms are just one area of potential confusion for a newcomer to the field, but get ready – there are more and they are not always so obvious! For example, there are various ways of describing a learner's L2 knowledge. As mentioned above, **interlanguage** is one name applied to the learner's system. Despite some concern over the way the term implicitly compares learner language to NS language, portraying the former as always incomplete and somehow 'less' than NS knowledge, it remains in wide use (see Chapter 3 for a discussion of the NS myth). Following Noam Chomsky, the distinction is often made between language **competence** (knowledge) and **performance** (use), with the latter being an imperfect representation of former. Other common terms include *proficiency, ability,* and the one I have been using here, *knowledge.* Part of this ambiguity comes from the elusiveness of the concept itself (just what *is* knowledge?), but it is also sometimes the result of dissatisfaction with previous terms. For instance, *competence* is often equated with a monolingual state of mind, thus **multicompetence** has been introduced by Vivian Cook (1991, 1992) as a way of describing the multilingual mind.

The word *competence* also provides an excellent example of the way a single term is sometimes used with different meanings. Traditionally, competence has suggested a fairly stable state of cognition – what a language user knows. In this view we can expect that at a certain point a learner will acquire, say, the past tense, and use it more or less reliably, recognizing when an error has occurred. For others, however, competence is seen as a largely social construction (remember the shift toward social theories in the 1990s?). A speaker may use his or her language in more or less 'competent' ways depending on the setting, topic, or interlocutor, thus rather than conceptualizing competence as a uniform, mental construct, we can see it as dynamic. Competence is continually recreated and co-constructed between conversational partners in interaction (Shea, 1994). As you become familiar with the various research paradigms in TESOL you will soon learn to recognize the way a particular scholar is positioning him or herself with regard to these and other concepts.

Conclusion

The goal of this chapter was to help you situate yourself, your discipline and your graduate program within a wider context in order to begin to get a better idea of what to expect from your MA experience. You can now see that you will encounter diverse perspectives, and you can understand, given the history of the field, why this is so. You should also be prepared to be taught to fish, rather than to be given a fish. In other words, your program will prepare you to draw on current theories and practices to develop an informed approach to teaching that will be further developed in a particular context as you reflect upon your own practice. Finally, we took some steps to prepare you not only for a diversity of perspectives in your study, but for a certain amount of inconsistency and ambiguity, as well. Armed now with this background, let's move on to Chapter 2, where we will delve into what you actually want to learn about: language, learning, and teaching.

Recommended reading

Howatt, A. P. R. with Widdowson, H. G. (2001). *A History of English Language Teaching*. Oxford: Oxford University Press.
Richards, J. C. and Rodgers, T. S. (2001). *Approaches and Methods in Language Teaching*. Cambridge: Cambridge University Press.

These two books provide clear, thorough overviews of the history of ELT. Howatt and Widdowson begin their discussion in 1400, while

Richards and Rodgers briefly review the methods of the 1800s before focusing on developments of the twentieth century.

Brown, H. D., Tarone, E., Swan, M., Ellis, R., Prodromou, L., Jung, U., Bruton, A. Johnson, K., Nunan, D., Oxford, R. L., Goh, C., Waters, A., and Savignon, S. J. (2006). Forty years of language teaching. *Language Teaching*, 40(2): 1–15.

While this article is not a substitute for either of the texts described above, it is an enjoyable complement, as each scholar tackles a single decade, starting with the 1960s and provides a personal view of what it was like to be a language teacher at that time.

Ramanathan, V. (2002). *The Politics of TESOL Education: Writing, Knowledge, Critical Pedagogy*. New York: RoutledgeFalmer.

Ramanathan's examination of the situated nature of knowledge in TESOL provides new students with critical insights into their own program and learning. This study extends the work of Ramanathan, Davies, and Schleppegrell (2001), discussed in this chapter.

Richards, J. and Schmidt, R. (2002). *Dictionary of Language Teaching and Applied Linguistics*. 3rd edition, Harlow: Longman.

An up-to-date dictionary of applied linguistics will help you decipher the concepts and terminology you will encounter in your reading. In addition to definitions, you will often also find citations for key scholars and publications relating to each entry.

Activities

1. Consider the context in which you plan to teach ESL (type of students, region, type of school). What do you think you will need to know to help your students learn? Which of the items on your list do you think are most important? Compare your list to that of someone who plans to teach in a different context. What differences are there between your lists and why do you think they are there?

2. It can often take up to two years for a journal article to be published, so discussion of the most up-to-date research findings, pedagogical recommendations, and controversies and concerns in the field are usually presented at conferences. Take a look

at presentation titles and abstracts from conferences where language acquisition and pedagogy are the focus (see the suggested sites below). What kinds of issues are discussed? What academic perspectives are represented?

International Association of Applied Linguistics: www.aila.info
International Association of Teachers of English as a Foreign
    Language: www.iatefl.org
Teachers of English to Speakers of Other Languages: www.tesol.org
American Association for Applied Linguistics: www.aaal.org
Australian Council of TESOL Associations: www.tesol.org.au
British Association for Applied Linguistics: www.baal.org.uk

3. Find two or three of the articles that were provided as examples of different types of applied linguistic research and compare them. What kind of information is provided about the study participants in each article? What kind of research questions are asked? What is provided as evidence to support the findings of the study? How are the articles structured?

2
Language, Learning, and Teaching

In the previous chapter I emphasized the variation that exists among TESOL practitioners, but in this chapter we will focus on our common knowledge base: language, teaching, and learning. As noted in Chapter 1, teaching is not simply a matter of imitating or avoiding the actions of other instructors we have observed. Good teaching requires a great deal of technical, specialized knowledge: an understanding of the structure and functions of language, of general principles of learning, of how languages are acquired, and, yes, of pedagogical principles. This chapter will introduce you to a variety of theoretical perspectives and current thinking on language, learning, and teaching.

What is language?

This must seem not only a ridiculous, but a somewhat disappointing question with which to begin, rather like asking students in an MA program in math to begin the course by practicing their multiplication tables. Yet, as it turns out, this is a question to which there is not one clear response, as there is for 2×2. At the same time, it is important to consider what language is, in order to be able to teach it. Your view of language will have direct implications for your classroom practice. For example, if you see language as a set of rules, you will likely give prominence to the regularities of language, conveying these to your students and perhaps helping them to discover these rules for themselves. Below is a list of definitions of language. Before considering them, you may want to try to work out your own view of what language is.

1. 'Language is a purely human and non-instinctive method of communicating ideas, emotions and desires by means of voluntarily produced symbols.' (Edward Sapir, 1921, p. 8)
2. 'A language is a system of arbitrary vocal symbols by means of which a social group co-operates.' (Bernard Bloch and George Trager, 1942, p. 5)
3. A language is 'a set (finite or infinite) of sentences, each finite in length and constructed out of a finite set of elements.' (Noam Chomsky, 1957/2002, p. 13)
4. Language is 'a range of possibilities, an open-ended set of options in behavior that are available to the individual...' (M. A. K. Halliday, 1973, p. 41)
5. 'Grammar is... simply the name for certain categories of observed repetitions in discourse. There is no natural fixed structure to language.' (Paul Hopper, 1998, p. 156)
6. Languages are 'the sedimented products of repeated acts of identity.' (Alastair Pennycook, 2004, p. 15)
7. 'There is, or at least there may well be, no such thing as English.... A language, in short, is ultimately a collection of ideolects which have been determined to belong together for what are ultimately non-and extra-linguistic reasons.' (Timothy Reagan, 2004, p. 42)
8. Language is 'a process in which we participate.' (Diane Larsen-Freeman and Lynne Cameron, 2008, p. 109)

• What similarities do you see among the definitions? What differences?
• How do the definitions change over time?

The introduction to the history of the field from the previous chapter should have prepared you to make a few comments on these definitions. For example, you may have noticed how they change through time. We begin with language as a pre-existing entity, with the first three focusing on language as an abstract system. **Halliday**, then, recognizes language as structure, but emphasizes its function, seeing it instead as a flexible resource for making meaning. Definitions 5–7 exhibit the mark of poststructuralism and postmodernism, as language is no longer seen as a fixed object, but as social action. You might also note the move away from attempts to delineate the purposes for which language is used; in fact, only Sapir uses the word 'communication.' While communicating is certainly something we do with language, it is absent in definitions such as **Chomsky's**, because his interest lies in laying bare the structure of language. Sociocultural theorists recognize that language is the means by which we accomplish much of our lives. We reconstruct ourselves, others, and our relationships through language, as well as reconstructing language itself each time we use it, thus to describe language only in terms of a communicative device obscures its wider significance.

Halliday (2004/1969) acknowledged the frustration that language educators feel when they meet up with so many definitions that vary so widely. Yet, he pointed out, too, that the question 'what is language?' is not as straightforward as it may seem, and that 'the only satisfactory response is "why do you want to know?"' (p. 269). On the one hand, our response to 'why do you want to know?' will be 'to teach ESL.' However, what aspect of ESL we teach differs with and even within each lesson, thus the question must constantly be revisited. At times we need to focus on structure, emphasizing, as Linell puts it, 'what can be said within in a particular language system' (1998, p. 3). Our students need and want to learn the patterns and regularities in form that exist at all levels of language: sounds (**phonology**), words and the ways in which they are formed (lexical **semantics, morphology**), sentence patterns (**syntax**), the ways in which sentences create coherent wholes (**discourse**), and the ways in which interlocutors make sense of language and use conventions of appropriacy (**pragmatics**).

Yet, students cannot simply be taught an abstract system, but must recognize that language is a way of making meaning and constructing understandings among speakers, and that choices in language use shape and are shaped by context, in what is known as a dialogical relationship. In other words, we *choose* our language according to the physical setting, time of day, conversational goals, and participant characteristics and social relationships. At the same time, the language we use also *creates* this context. For example, a formal situation can become much less formal when one person tells a risqué joke. With regard to educational contexts, the unequal power relationship that often exists between students and teachers is constructed through, for example, the kinds of questions that teachers often ask students – that is, those for which the answer is already known by the teacher. In these choices, too, there are regularities, but unlike the rules that govern language structure, rules of use tend to work more as guidelines, and not subscribing to them usually results in social awkwardness, as when one person is seen as rude or overly friendly. As described in the previous chapter, these patterns of language features that cluster together both in response to and as a way of constructing a particular language-using situation are referred to as **genres**.

Halliday's functional (as opposed to formal) perspective on language, from which the study of genre grew, also requires us to see language as both a system and a process. In this view, we must not only note the features of language, and the immediate social context of language use, but its relationship to the larger social system that it simultaneously creates as meanings are selected. Language, seen broadly as text and genre, both constructs and is constructed through culture (Martin and Rose, 2008). This has important implications for teachers, as certain genres are powerful and privileged, yet access to them is not necessarily equal for all language users. Increasing awareness of and access to generic conventions has become a priority in many countries, and as a result sophisticated pedagogies that draw on this view of language have been developed (see, e.g., Feez, 1998).

In addition to considering the nature of language, as ESL teachers we can also ask the more specific question 'what is English?' However, far from simplifying our definitional project, this question actually raises new concerns, as up to now we have ignored a crucial issue for English language educators: varieties of English. A dialect, or language variety, can differ at any of the levels described above: pronunciation, vocabulary, syntax, discourse, or pragmatics. (Note that although when we speak of different accents, this refers solely to phonological differences, that is, variations in pronunciation.) English is widely used, and countless local dialects and professional **registers** exist. Which variety (or varieties) should an instructor choose to teach?

Practical considerations come into play. As the instructor, you cannot be expected to be an expert in Canadian, Australian, and

Singaporean English; therefore, your choice will be restricted by your familiarity with different varieties. The purposes for which your students are learning English will also need to be considered. Do most students need the kind of English that will allow them to pass a college entrance exam, or will they likely be working in an environment where English is the main medium of communication? Will they be speaking largely with native speakers from the US or will they tend to interact more in an international community made up of other L2 users? Your choice might also be affected by social and political considerations from outside the classroom. Texts that present only one variety of English may be mandated by the school or government; indeed, a language variety may be imposed explicitly by law or implicitly through the expectations of parents and school administrators who see a particular variety of English as a tool for success.

Yet language is more than a mere 'tool' for communication. This often used metaphor presents language as neutral, working pretty much the same way for everyone who uses it, much the way nearly anyone with a bit of arm strength can use a hammer to pound in nails. Indeed, as abstract systems, linguists recognize that all languages are equal in the sense that we can communicate any idea in any language. Certainly, some concepts that are encapsulated in a single word in one language may require a paragraph to explain in another, but this does not make that language impoverished, as the idea can still be conveyed. Socially, however, it is far from the case that languages are seen as equal; some languages and language varieties are regarded as more prestigious than others. The tool metaphor obscures this, as well as the ways that L2 users and speakers of minority or non-standard varieties of English are often not treated as legitimate speakers (Bourdieu, 1977; Lippi-Green, 1997; Miller, 2004). Thus, the choice of which variety of English to teach involves not only practical, but also ideological considerations.

With regard to English, the prestige varieties are generally those spoken by NSs in countries that Kachru and Nelson (1996) have referred to as 'inner circle countries,' where English is the primary language, such as Australia, Canada, the UK, and the US. Yet, as Henry Widdowson (1994) points out, it is certainly not just any NS who is envisioned as a model. Regardless of the preferences of the learners themselves, schools are unlikely to imagine ethnic or regional varieties, such as African-American vernacular English or the English of the Southern US, as models when they say that they are teaching 'American English.' Some may see these types of English, however, as more 'authentic' than the varieties used in multilingual countries, such India, Nigeria, and Singapore, where English is widely used, but generally not spoken natively. Kachru and Nelson call these 'outer circle' countries. In these contexts, even though English has developed into a distinct variety, it is generally not viewed as a legitimate model for learning. Thus, it is equally unlikely that a school in Japan would advocate the teaching of, for example, Zambian English. Countries such as Korea, where English is mainly learned in an educational context and used in limited domains, have been called 'expanding circle' countries by Kachru and Nelson. In fact, this prejudice against ethnic and regional variation often extends even to schools located in the areas where one of these varieties is widely used. Thus, ESL students in a school with, say, a predominately African-American population will likely be discouraged from acquiring features of that variety, despite its prevalence in their community.

The reflexive exclusion from the classroom of so many varieties of English sets up a very small minority of the world's population as authentic and legitimate models of language use. This runs the risk of disengaging our students, who are asked to reach for an unattainable model and one over which they feel no sense of ownership. As Widdowson (1994) explains,

> If natural language learning depends on asserting some ownership over the language, this cannot be promoted by means of language which is authentic only because it belongs to somebody else and expresses somebody else's identity.
>
> (p. 387)

Holding up a limited group of NSs as models of English may not only intimidate and alienate many learners, but is also likely to give them a distorted view of the way English is used today. (See Chapter 3 for problems with the idea of the 'native speaker,' a term I have thus far used uncritically.)

L2 users of English far outnumber NSs today and their numbers will likely continue to grow (Graddol, 1999; Crystal, 2008). Most communication in English takes place between L2 users, rather than between

NSs and NNSs, thus making it more reasonable in many teaching contexts to use proficient, intelligible L2 speakers as the norm. Because of these developments, interest in teaching English as an international language (EIL) or English as a **lingua franca** (ELF) has been growing, and research that can be used as a pedagogical basis for teaching global varieties is well underway (House, 1999; Jenkins, 2000, 2002; Seidlhofer, 2004). In addition, calls have been put forth for education that helps NSs gain a greater awareness of international norms of English language use as a way of reducing what is often the marginalization of NNSs, as well as to facilitate intercultural communication (e.g., Lin et al., 2002).

These ideas resonate, too, in primary and secondary classrooms where English is taught mainly to immigrant children. Here teachers are more likely to choose a NS model appropriate for the region, usually the one perceived as the 'standard.' Yet this should not preclude classroom explorations of varieties that are perceived as less prestigious, and even in these contexts successful, but not necessarily native-like L2 use may be held up as a goal. The desire for raising NS awareness of global varieties of English has extended to state school contexts, as well (Kubota, 2001).

So, while you have started your program with a plan to teach English, you can now see that this is a multifaceted proposition and many factors, both practical and ideological, will come into play in deciding the variety or varieties to teach. You will need to achieve a balance of finding an appropriate model, while also acknowledging the legitimacy of other Englishes. With language itself such a complicated entity, you can guess that learning will be no less so.

How do we learn (language)?

The short answer to the question that opens this section is that we do not know. Or, more accurately, I could say that we know bits and pieces, but not precisely how they all fit together. In order to prepare you for your meeting with these bits and pieces, take a moment to think about how you conceptualize learning:

- How do you define 'learning'? To what extent does learning occur internally (in the brain) and to what extent is it an external (social, environmental) process?

- How do students demonstrate learning?
- How is learning a language similar to learning other things? How is it different? Think about the learning of a skill, such as swimming, or an academic subject, such as history.
- What are some differences between learning a first or second language as a child and learning a second language as an adult?

A recent edited collection (VanPatten and Williams, 2007) contains nine chapters, each describing a different current theory of second language acquisition. If we asked the SLA scholars who wrote these chapters to respond to these questions, they would not all have the same answers. You may want to come back to these questions when you have finished this section to see if you can figure out how a researcher from each of the perspectives discussed below might respond. I have selected just four perspectives – the innatist position, the interaction hypothesis, sociocultural theory, and emergentism – to discuss here as a way of demonstrating the breadth of theoretical approaches to SLA.

Innatist perspectives

An innatist perspective on SLA differs from the theories discussed below in that, rather than attempting to explain the process by which L2 development occurs, its goal is to describe the learner's mental representation of the L2 (see **Chomsky**'s definition of language at the beginning of this chapter). In other words, the theory is concerned solely with understanding **competence**, rather than **performance**. The theory draws on Chomsky's (1965) construct of Universal Grammar (UG), which was originally applied to the understanding of L1 acquisition as a way of explaining the observation that children's grammars are far more complex than could be expected given the **poverty of the stimulus** they receive. While adults do adjust their language when talking with children, Chomsky described their speech as 'impoverished,' suggesting that it rarely contains complete sentences and instead often offers fragments, false starts, and ungrammatical language from which he believed it would be difficult to derive a full grammar, as children do. This led him to conclude that language learning is different from other types of learning and must be aided by an innate faculty, called UG, which sharply restricts the forms that grammars can take. With the help of this innate knowledge of the possibilities of grammar, relatively little input can be used to set the parameters of the particular L1 to which the child is exposed. As an example of one of these parameters, English does not allow its users to drop subject pronouns, whereas Spanish does. Thus, in English 'Dances beautifully' is not a possible variation on 'He dances beautifully,' but in Spanish both options are grammatical. Through input alone, UG allows a child to switch the pro-drop parameter to the appropriate setting.

For researchers working within this paradigm, it is generally accepted that UG is still accessible for the learning of additional languages in early childhood, making their acquisition and ultimate attainment in the **target language** similar to that in the native language. However, as anyone who has undertaken the study of an L2 as an adult is painfully aware, the outcomes for learners later in life rarely reach the point at which they become indistinguishable from NSs. (Although note that the process is neither quick nor painless for children learning their first language, who are treated with great leniency for the many years they spend in the learning process. See Chapter 2 for more on age and SLA.)

The difficulty most adult learners have in acquiring highly advanced L2 proficiency raises the question of whether access to UG remains available throughout one's life (as adult L2 learners still develop a grammar that goes beyond what could have been predicted from the input), is available only up until a certain age, or remains accessible, but only partially. Each of these positions has consequences for pedagogy. Clearly, from a UG perspective input is important, but if UG remains accessible, pedagogical intervention will do little to alter the rate or route of acquisition. If access is blocked, however, instruction and feedback will play an important role. The issue is difficult to address, as it requires separating the learning done via UG from learning that occurs through general principles.

Lydia White (1989, 2003), Kevin Gregg (1996), and Suzanne Flynn (Flynn and Lust, 2002) are a few influential names associated with this theoretical perspective. The primary research methodology used to investigate the role of UG in SLA is grammaticality judgment tasks, which provide data as to the learner's perceptions of what is (not) possible in the target language. Work in this area can be quite technical, and a solid grounding in Chomsky's theory of syntax, as well as knowledge of how previous evidence has been variously interpreted is necessary for understanding current research. However, for those seeking to examine such scholarship, White (1985) is an excellent example of research methodology and, as an early work, assumptions and findings are more accessible than current work for those without a great deal of background. Also worth examining is Flynn and Martohardjono (1995), who briefly survey the background of UG-driven research in order to reach some pedagogical implications, which are rarely discussed from this perspective.

The interaction hypothesis

Whereas the goal of the previous theory was to describe the learner's mental representation of language, the next three perspectives seek to understand how language learning occurs. In an interactionist approach to SLA, social interaction is seen as a necessary factor for learning, as it provides data, which the learner then processes internally. This line of research developed from Evelyn Hatch's (1978) proposal that SLA grows out of the need to communicate, as well as from the attention that **Krashen** drew to the role of comprehensible **input**. The communication breakdowns that occur more frequently in conversations involving a NNS are thought to be a key catalyst for learning because they force speakers to pause from their conversation in order to reach an understanding of the meaning of a particular utterance. In doing so one or both conversational partners must change their utterance, for example, by choosing different words, by articulating more clearly, or by changing the sentence structure. This is referred to as '**negotiation** for meaning.' In an important revision of the interaction hypothesis, Michael Long, an influential proponent of this perspective, described the importance of this thus:

> *negotiation for meaning*, and especially negotiation work that triggers *interactional* adjustments by the NS or more competent interlocutor, facilitates acquisition because it connects input, internal learner capacities, particularly selective attention, and output in productive ways.
>
> (1996, pp. 451–2; italics in original)

Thus linguistic input, output, feedback, and attention are important components of this model of SLA.

Input is a crucial source of information for the learner regarding what is possible in the target language. In other words, it provides **positive evidence** about the language. Researchers have been particularly interested in the changes that are made to NS speech that is directed to NNSs, referred to as **modified input** (Pica, 1994; Gass, 1997). The language may be simplified, for example, by drawing from a restricted vocabulary or avoiding complex sentence structures. It may also be elaborated, such as when the speaker provides more information, for example, by describing in detail a particular referent (changing 'it' to 'standard poodle') or a lexical item (replacing 'standard poodle' with 'a very intelligent breed of dog that often has pom-poms on its head and tail'). A learner is able to get modified input by signaling a lack of comprehension.

Learners, too, formulate utterances that are difficult for their interlocutors to interpret, and in this case they, too, are made aware of this through feedback. Explicit feedback (e.g., 'No. The correct pronunciation is ...') occurs more often in classroom contexts, but not all feedback to learners is explicit, nor does it always identify the precise location or nature of the breakdown. Both in and out of the classroom L2 learners also receive implicit feedback in the form of requests for clarification ('Excuse me?'), confirmation checks ('Do you mean ...?'), and comprehension checks ('Are you following me?'). **Recasts** are another type of implicit feedback in which the learner's ungrammatical utterance is reformulated by his or her interlocutor:

S: The boy have many flowers in the basket.
T: Yes, the boy has many flowers in the basket.
                          (Nicholas, Lightbown, and Spada, 2001, p. 721)

Implicit feedback, and recasts in particular, have received a great deal of attention from scholars who recognize their importance not only for researchers seeking to understand SLA, but for teachers who struggle daily with whether and how to provide feedback to their learners (Lyster, 1998; Nicholas, Lightbown, and Spada, 2001; Leeman, 2003; Mackey, 2006).

Feedback can show the learner what is *not* possible in the target language. In the face of this **negative evidence**, learners must modify their utterances, thinking of new ways to express their meaning, forcing them to produce what Swain (1985) referred to as 'pushed' output. It is thought that output can play an important role in helping the learner notice L2 form-meaning relationships and eventually to produce more complex and accurate language. At the same time, output creates a potentially positive loop, in which the learner is able to try out new forms, receive feedback on them, and try again. Note, however, my use of the word 'can' at the start of this paragraph. While negotiation offers opportunities for learners to notice differences between their own language use and that of the other speaker, and to make use of what they have noticed, processing constraints, such as our limited memory, ensure that this does not always happen. Learning about the conditions under which learner's attention is or can be drawn to L2 forms is of great interest to both L2 teachers and researchers (Philp, 2003; Mackey, 2006).

In addition to the works cited in this section and in the related discussion in Chapter 1, readers may look to Gass and Mackey (2006) for a clear and concise overview of this theoretical perspective. In addition, note that, as mentioned in Chapter 1, the interactionist position has been closely tied to pedagogical concerns, with the same tasks that are used in research also being employed by teachers. The pedagogical use of tasks is discussed in further detail below, in the section on teaching.

Sociocultural theory

Rather than viewing interaction as a site for the learner to obtain samples of the target language which can then be processed internally, a sociocultural view of SLA posits that it is *in* the social interaction that development occurs and that development is inseparable from its context. Rather than being an individual property housed in a learner's mind, as the previous two perspectives suggest, knowledge is also social, arising from the context. The context itself is constructed not only through interpersonal, but also historical processes. Learning is defined as changes in behavior that move the learner toward greater independence.

The work of Russian psychologist **Lev Vygotsky** figures prominently in the research of sociocultural theorists. It is somewhat surprising that sociocultural theory was taken up rather belatedly by applied linguists in comparison to others in education, as language itself plays such a significant role in this theory. One important tenet of the theory is that humans do not interact directly with the world. Instead, they bring about changes through the use of physical and symbolic tools, which mediate their interaction with the world. Language is the prominent symbolic tool for supporting (mediating) our own behavior. This is demonstrated in child development by Vygotsky (1978) in an experiment in which three- and four-year-old children attempted to get at some candy that had been placed high up in a cupboard. A stool and stick were in the room. Speech seemed to help the children solve the problem of getting the candy. They initially described and analyzed the situation, then moved on to planning their action aloud, and eventually continued to talk themselves through the actions to successfully reach the candy.

According to Vygotsky, initially, many of our actions are 'other-regulated.' Younger children, for example, may not have been able to figure out how to obtain the candy themselves, but could have followed instructions on how to do so. With further development we move toward 'self-regulation,' which is what the three- and four-year-olds were doing. We may continue to do this as adults – we usually call it talking to ourselves! Eventually this 'private speech' becomes 'inner speech.' At this stage of development, mental processes are internalized and we are able to regulate our behavior without using the actual spoken forms of language. A challenging task, however, may require us to again externalize our mental processes. For example, sometimes after I have been mulling over a problem and decide to ask someone for help, I often realize the answer simply through the process of describing the problem aloud. In terms of L2 learning, 'to be an advanced speaker/user of a language means to be able to control one's psychological and social activity through the language' (Lantolf, 2000, p. 6). Proficiency means self-regulation.

Another important construct within sociocultural theory is the **zone of proximal development** (ZPD), defined by Vygotsky as 'the distance between the actual developmental level [of an individual] as determined by independent problem solving and the level of potential development' (1978, p. 86). This is a metaphorical space in which an individual's abilities are stretched beyond what he or she can achieve alone. Physical artifacts, such as the stool and stick from the experiment above, may help, but frequently the construction of the ZPD has been investigated in terms of collaborative human activity. The collaboration that assists the learner in filling this gap is called **scaffolding**. Traditionally, an expert–novice relationship was thought to be necessary for learning in the ZPD, as the more capable participant could provide assistance; however, examinations of learner–learner interaction in L2 classrooms has shown that peers are able to scaffold each other (Donato, 1994; Ohta, 1995).

Because the theory is a relative newcomer to our field, the pedagogical implications of a sociocultural theory of SLA have yet to be explored to a great extent (although see Lantolf and Thorne, 2006; Lantolf and Poehner, 2008). As with the interaction hypothesis, further research should help us, as teachers, identify means of recognizing and providing assistance that is appropriate to a learner's developmental level and constructing classroom activities that encourage the kind of peer collaboration that will also support learning. James Lantolf has been central in bringing sociocultural theory into SLA research and his edited collection (2000) provides an excellent introduction to many of the scholars doing significant work in this area. Also, Foster and Ohta (2005) is helpful for teasing out the differences between interactionist and sociocultural perspectives, as they integrate the two in a description of peer collaboration.

Emergentism

The emergentist perspective provides a new way of looking at language, as exemplified in the quote from linguist Paul Hopper, at the start of this chapter: 'Grammar is … simply the name for certain categories of observed repetitions in discourse. There is no natural fixed structure to language' (1998, p. 156). Hopper shifted our view of language from a set of forms existing outside ourselves that we draw on to make meaning, to an understanding of linguistic forms as continually constructed through discourse, contingent upon context, and always negotiated among speakers. Thus, in using language we also change it, a fact that applies as much to L2 learners as it does to NSs.

In contrast to the interactionist position, which is moving ever closer to gaining the status of a theory, emergentism, still in its infancy, is far from having an all-encompassing theory of SLA, but does have the advantage of a clear, strong thesis and research program (O'Grady, 2008). Emergentists reject the idea of an innate module in the mind that is responsible for the development of language (UG, as discussed above). Instead, both the form and acquisition of language are best explained by reference to more basic non-linguistic (i.e., 'non-grammatical') factors and their interaction – physiology, perception, processing, working memory, pragmatics, social interaction, properties of the input, the learning mechanisms, and so on.

(O'Grady, 2008, p. 448)

This view leaves space for examination of the structure of the brain and its processing mechanisms, as well as environmental and social considerations.

Without an innate language faculty to explain SLA, emergentists see language acquisition as a matter of using generalized learning mechanisms (those that are also employed in other types of learning) to uncover statistical regularities – to determine frequencies and distributions of particular forms – in the language they encounter. They posit that these mechanisms can be quite simple. The complexity of language learning derives not from the complexity of the processing mechanism, but from the complexity of the environment, in which physical, social, cognitive, emotional, and historical factors interact. Language acquisition, then, is based on the sum total of the learner's previous encounters with the language: 'The knowledge underlying fluent, systematic, apparently rule-governed use of language is the learner's entire collection of memories of previously experienced utterances' (N. Ellis and Larsen-Freeman, 2006, p. 565).

Of particular importance in this quote is the use of the phrase '*apparently* rule governed' to describe language use. Recall Hopper's assertion that 'there is no natural fixed structure to language.' Rules are not the *cause* of the systematic language-using behaviors we can observe, but rather the regularities emerge *from* the behavior, which is constrained in particular ways by the environment. Nick Ellis points out that 'although language behavior can be described as being rule-like, this does not imply that language behavior is rule-governed' (N. Ellis, 1998, p. 638). He uses an analogy to traffic to illustrate this:

> Consider a case of emergent systematicity: the growth of queues at traffic lights on a multi-lane highway. The longer the lights have been red, the longer the queues. The greater the volume of traffic, the longer the queues. So far, so obvious. But, more interesting, typically the lengths of the queues in the various lanes are roughly equal. There is no prescription to this effect in the Highway Code.

Instead, the 'rule' that equalizes the number of cars in the carriage-ways emerges from satisfying the constraints of the more basic goals and behaviors of drivers, traffic planners, cars and time.

(1998, p. 643)

For this example, what looks like a rule is actually the result of, among other things, each driver independently selecting a particular lane.

For a language example, let's consider text messages, which, although relatively new, exhibit an abbreviated style that make their genre readily identifiable. These regularities are not the result of their users following a texting manual that explains that most vowels should be omitted and that they should use 'btw' instead of the entire phrase 'by the way.' Instead, these rule-like conventions have been shaped by the medium, which limits the length of the message. In addition, the cost of a text message is normally much less than a phone call, thus many people prefer to hold conversations this way, making speed important when replying, again encouraging short forms. Thus, what appears to be rule-governed behavior is really a flexible set of conventions that have *emerged* in interaction with factors as diverse as technological limitations, financial considerations, and time constraints.

Thus, from this perspective, learning is a matter of perceiving and processing linguistic input, but it is also driven by non-linguistic factors, of which cognitive considerations are only one. Larsen-Freeman and Cameron (2008) emphasize this point:

Learning is not the taking in of linguistic forms by learners, but the constant adaptation of their linguistic resources in the service of meaning-making in response to the affordances that emerge in the communicative situation, which is, in turn, affected by the learners' adaptability.

(p. 135)

In other words, each communicative situation, such as a text message, offers, as well as constrains, different possibilities (or affordances) for language use. The language learner's use results from the interaction of a number of factors, including the message, the context, and the mutual shaping of the context by the interlocutors.

If language is learned through the same generalized learning mechanism used for acquiring other skills, how might we explain the difficulties that many adult L2 learners have in acquiring a version of the target language that is indistinguishable from NS varieties? Nativists, for instance, are able to explain this as a lack of access to UG. Emergentists, on the other hand, note that the frequency of certain forms in one's native language allows for predictability and thus fluent use, but this same frequency poses a challenge for acquisition of an L2. This is because the most frequently used forms tend to become phonologically reduced (consider how 'I don't know' often becomes 'I-oh-no,' or even simply a sort of humming of the intonation contour), which in turn makes their grammatical construction more difficult to perceive. This means that they occur, in the perception of the learner, with less frequency than do content words. Thus, adults who learn an L2 without instruction often use a form of language that exhibits content words, such as nouns and verbs, but with little or inconsistent use of the less salient elements that carry grammatical information, such as verb endings for tense and agreement (see N. Ellis, 2008 for a thorough explanation of this cycle).

Emergentism seems to suggest exciting avenues for exploring L2 development in a way that privileges neither the cognitive nor the social, but recognizes learning as the complex interaction of these, as well as other factors. Although we remain far from being able to provide a full emergentist account of SLA, let alone one that might be of use to teachers, Larsen-Freeman and Cameron's (2008, Chapter 7) discussion of the ways in which a view of the L2 classroom based on complexity theory (a perspective related to emergentism) might change our approach to teaching offers some initial thoughts in this direction. Some scholars remain cautious in their assessment of emergentism, wary that it merely provides a new metaphor for language acquisition, rather than a truly new approach. It is worth stepping back for a moment to consider the role of metaphor in constructing understanding in general, and specifically with regard to studying and describing learning.

Conceptualizing learning

Metaphors reflect and shape how we see the world. In doing so they can help us understand difficult phenomena and spur innovation by opening up new possibilities for viewing familiar objects and activities, but at the same time, they can lead us to expect only a narrower set of possible behaviors – those that fit within the metaphor – and thus restrict our thinking. Anna Sfard (1998) illustrates how this works using two metaphors for learning: the acquisition metaphor and the participation metaphor. The first is and has long been dominant. Within the acquisition metaphor, learning is seen as 'getting something.' That 'something' may be knowledge, ideas, conccpts, or, of course, language. This can be seen clearly when students suddenly understand and they cry out, 'I *get* it!' or 'I *have* the answer!' Some views of learning, such as the innatist model, are quite clearly built on the acquisition metaphor, using verbs such as these (or their more formal counterparts, such as 'acquire') to describe learning. As Sfard points out, more recent theories that describe learners as 'constructing' knowledge, often through collaboration with others, still rely on the acquisition metaphor. Although these perspectives see the learner in more active ways (building the knowledge themselves, rather than having it given to them by a teacher), they are still seen as doing so in the interest of making a 'thing' their own.

The participation metaphor, of which sociocultural theory is a good example, is newer and conceptualizes learning as doing or being. Rather than existing as an object (knowledge) to obtain, action is emphasized (knowing). When *having* something gives way to *doing* something, learning is understood as changes in the nature of an individual's participation as he or she becomes a part of a new community. Learning, then, is becoming part of something greater. Knowing is in flux and we do not expect to see it performed in the same way all the time, as we do with knowledge. Knowing is thus context-dependent in a way that the more static knowledge is not. As Sfard is careful to emphasize, participation is a metaphor and not synonymous with classroom approaches that encourage students to interact (participate!) in the construction of knowledge. As pointed out above, many of these perspectives, while ascribing to the importance of participation in the sense of interaction, also subscribe to the acquisition metaphor, as they see participation as a way of gaining individual knowledge. The participation metaphor emphasizes community and the links between the individual and the community, where knowledge is communal and distributed among members. Sfard uses a living organism as a metaphor for understanding the participation metaphor, explaining that it implies that the identity of an individual, like an identity of a living organ, is a function of his or her being (or becoming) a part of a greater entity. Thus, talk about the 'stand-alone learner' and 'decontextualized learning' becomes as pointless as the attempts to define lungs or muscles without a reference to the living body within which they both exist and function.

(1998, p. 6)

Thus, rather than implying a specific way of teaching (say, encouraging talk among students), each metaphor suggests a particular way of answering the question, 'what is learning?' (Sfard, 1998, p. 7).

An examination of the four theories described above should make it clear that an innatist perspective follows the acquisition metaphor. In this view language is an entity to be acquired by the individual. Sociocultural theory, on the other hand, draws largely from the participation metaphor, describing learning as changes in behavior and emphasizing the communal nature of knowledge. Interactionists largely draw on the acquisition metaphor, but have been moving more recently toward greater recognition of the possibilities that viewing learning from a new perspective can yield. Merrill Swain, for example, who originally used the term 'output' (1985), has more recently moved away from the acquisition metaphor and toward the participation metaphor, using the term 'languaging,' which she selected because, although it focuses on output, it does so without the use of the computer metaphor: 'For me, it conveyed an action – a dynamic, never-ending process of using language to make meaning' (Swain, 2006, p. 96). Sfard argues that both metaphors have value for helping us conceptualize learning, and emergentism may be the perspective that comes closest to integrating the two. From this view, it is more accurate to refer to use/learning rather than one or the other.

The metaphors we use to visualize learning also have consequences for our teaching, and it is to pedagogy that we now turn at last.

How do we teach language?

As you can tell from the previous section, we are not yet able (nor are we likely to be able in the near future) to base our pedagogy on a single theory of language learning. Fortunately, teachers have been coping with this situation for centuries – and in fact, even when presented with a unified theory and a set of principles to follow, few have done so consistently and to the letter. Experience tells teachers that they need to adapt, and they do. The question of how to teach is one to which you probably have more easily accessible opinions than you may have had for language or learning, having probably selected your graduate program with ideas of learning about *teaching* to a greater extent than about language or learning. In addition, in your role as a student, you have observed classroom teaching much of your life, and you likely have memories of particularly stellar instructors whom you hope to emulate, as well as plans to avoid the behaviors of those whose classroom performances were boring or even painful. Let's take a moment to consider your views on teaching, keeping in mind the ways that these prior experiences might color your ideas:

- What is your definition of 'good' teaching?
- What are the most important qualities of a 'good' teacher? Of a 'good' student?
- What is the teacher's role in the classroom? What is the student's?
- How do you think language learning in a classroom differs from language learning without formal instruction?

In Chapter 1, I mentioned two points that are worth reiterating again here. First, I warned against expecting to simply be given a set of procedures to follow when teaching. Second, I emphasized the value of teachers' knowledge and their abilities to continually shape their pedagogy in response to their learners needs. You probably came up with a wide variety of responses to the question above, which signals the inadequacy of attempting to teach all learners through a single method, and suggests the need for teachers to instead base their practice on more flexible principles that they can enact as they see fit for different classes. This is the essence of the **postmethod** era in which we find ourselves at present. Below I highlight five facets of L2 pedagogy that I see as important: meaning/fluency, form/accuracy, autonomy, awareness, and opportunity.

Meaning/fluency

A legacy of Communicative Language Teaching, activities that focus on meaning remain a staple of the ESL classroom and are considered crucial for creating the conditions necessary for L2 development, particularly with respect to L2 comprehension and fluency (Long, 1996; DeKeyser, 1998). 'Meaning-based activities' refers here to those that encourage learners to focus their attention on achieving success-ful communication, more so than on the form that communication takes. Learners use their L2 resources to construct, modify, and inter-pret messages, actions that, you will recall, are thought to be impor-tant for facilitating acquisition, particularly from the interactionist position. Thus, open-ended activities like debates and discussions where learners share ideas and opinions are frequently used.

Many of the types of tasks often used by interactionist scholars to study negotiation of meaning have also emerged as useful pedagogi-cal devices because unlike in a discussion, they require an exchange of information for successful **task** completion. One example of an information gap task is the flower garden activity (Doughty and Pica, 1986), in which one speaker attempts to follow the instructions of his or her conversational partner to recreate a garden scene that is visible only to the person providing the instructions. As you may imagine, a great deal of meaning is **negotiated** as different colors and types of flowers and their specific locations are described. I have used a similar activity in written form by drawing a simple picture and writing detailed directions on how to replicate it. My students then work, sometimes in pairs, sometimes individually, to follow the instructions to try to create the same picture, which I only show to them once they have finished the task. This example also illustrates the often obscured point that 'communicative' is not equivalent to 'oral.' Reading and writing, too, involve communication and can be taught communicatively – that is, with a focus on the construction and interpretation of meaning.

Form/accuracy

In Chapter 1 we noted that Swain (1985) demonstrated that with-out explicit attention to form, learners may become fluent in the L2, but fail to develop grammatical accuracy. It is now widely accepted among researchers and practitioners of ELT that older learners and especially those who learn an L2 primarily within a classroom require **form-focused instruction** in order to develop high levels of gram-matical accuracy. Form-focused instruction, and particularly that which involves explicit attention to rules or forms, is an effective way of producing lasting changes in learners' language (Norris and

Ortega, 2000). Those who suffered through language classes in which they were required to memorize verb paradigms need not fear, however. Current approaches emphasize that such instruction should take place within activities that are meaningful to the learner. Note that the two information gap tasks described above (the flower garden and the drawing task) both implicitly require learners to attend to form within a communicative framework. Directional terms and prepositions indicating locations, for example, must be understood and used appropriately for success in both tasks, whereas in open-ended discussions learners may be able to avoid particular forms.

In addition to tasks that implicitly require a focus on form, **tasks that are designed to bring certain forms to learners' attention** can also be designed. One example is the dictogloss task (Wajnryb, 1990) in which a short text is read fairly quickly to students, who try to copy it as accurately as possible. After hearing it once or twice, they work in groups to try to reconstruct the exact text. This involves the learners in comparing their own output with that of others, and ultimately with the original text. Doing so helps them notice the differences and, as I have been delighted to note among my own students, the lively discussion that ensues on how to resolve these differences demonstrates a much higher level of engagement than students normally have with traditional grammar lessons. In addition, students are then eager to hear a grammatical rule to help them with their struggle (if they have not already discovered the rule on their own).

Another way to focus on form is in response to student errors, as part of a teacher's job is to provide feedback. Thus, a focus on form need not be planned as part of a stand-alone lesson, but can arise incidentally in communication with a student and then (possibly) be integrated into a larger lesson. In such spontaneous responses to learner talk the 'lesson' on L2 form takes place within a meaningful context. In addition, it is worth noting that while I have suggested that attention to meaning promotes fluency and attention to form promotes accuracy, a recent review suggests that the type of *integrated* form-focused instruction that we have just discussed can also have a positive effect on L2 fluency (Spada and Lightbown, 2008).

Autonomy

Promoting autonomy in language learning has become an important goal for many ELT practitioners. Autonomous learners are responsible for and in control of their own learning in the class, and ideally are able to employ strategies for learning outside the classroom as well. The move toward greater autonomy for language learners comes partly from the desire to help students manage their learning better, but also from a (potentially radical) recognition of what the learner brings to the educational situation. In this latter view, the teacher is no longer the center of the classroom, selecting activities and directing students, who are passive vessels waiting to be filled with the L2 (recall the acquisition metaphor). The idea is that learners who have greater control over what happens in the classroom will be more invested in their own learning – autonomous learners are motivated learners (for a review of research on autonomy, see Benson, 2007).

Strategy instruction (Oxford, 1990) is one way of increasing learner autonomy. For example, students might fill out a questionnaire that helps them uncover their beliefs about learning and their preferred learning strategies and, in doing so, become aware of others they might be able to use. Self-assessment is often used, and learners can also engage in self-directed learning by using new technologies, such as computer-assisted language learning (CALL) software, as well as free programs available on the internet. When autonomy is conceived of as a way of altering the balance of power in the classroom, learners are invited 'behind the scenes' as their instructor shares the goals and pedagogical rationale for certain activities with the students, something that seems to help even primary school-aged children take better advantage of language learning opportunities (Kolb, 2007). In fact, pushing this concept further, teachers can work together with students to negotiate the curriculum and means of assessment. Of course, students need support and guidance to become more autonomous in their learning, and Nunan (1995) suggests a step-by-step approach.

In some contexts autonomy may be more challenging to introduce than in others. In the US, for example, although the importance of individuality and student-directed learning are often talked about, in practice schools are faced with an increasingly homogenizing set of government assessments, and creating space for autonomy in this climate is a challenge (van Lier, 2007). In addition, the very idea of autonomy has been criticized as a Western-based concept, for what some have seen as an implicit representation of non-Western learners as passive and non-individualistic. Thus, as with all constructs, we must acknowledge its source and history, and work to create an autonomy that is contextually appropriate, rather than dictated by outsiders (Schmenk, 2005).

Language awareness

Similar to the way autonomy has been conceived, language awareness, which refers to explicit knowledge about language, comes in two main versions. The first derives largely from the interactionist perspective, where the noticing of L2 forms is seen as crucial to L2 development. The teaching of pragmatics, much of which involves learning what forms are appropriate under what conditions, has also been recognized as an area where learner attention needs to be drawn to form-function relationships. The second version, which is often referred to as *critical* language awareness, is concerned with power relations and the ways that these are constructed through language. From this perspective, learners are not presented with language as neutral, but rather they examine the ways that it constructs power and can be used to reproduce inequalities. Identity is central, and language learning is seen as a process of helping learners appropriate the L2 and use it to construct L2 selves with which they are at ease (for a broad review of language awareness research, see Svalberg, 2007).

Dictogloss, described above, is one example of an awareness-raising activity in the first vein in that it focuses learners' attention on language forms and creates a great deal of metalinguistic talk. Exercises that require learners to analyze language collaboratively in order to abstract a particular rule also increase language awareness in this sense. For example, given appropriate samples of language, learners can deduce, with no help from the teacher, that it is the length of an adjective in English that determines the type of comparative form that is used (e.g., 'smarter than' vs. 'more intelligent than'). Activities designed to raise *critical* language awareness also tend to be analytic and exploratory. Learners might, for example, engage in discussions of varieties of native and non-native accents in English, how these are perceived, and what the consequences of accented speech can be for learners. Social justice is an important part of critical language awareness, and the goal of this activity might be to help students develop speaking strategies not only for comprehensibility, but for expressing resistance to views based on accent prejudice.

Because of the discomfort learners may have employing forms of politeness that are different from their L1 (as a native speaker of English I have never quite gotten used to the formal French *vous*), **pragmatic** and sociolinguistic norms are often taught using awareness-raising activities. One way *not* to do this would be to tell learners that they must respond to a compliment by deflecting it (e.g., 'I love your shirt!' 'Thanks. It was a gift from my mother.'), as most middle-class Americans do. Instead, learners could collect and analyze compliment responses, and compare them to the way that they might respond in their native language. In this way, their consciousness about social uses of language is raised, but the forms become part of an array of choices they can make.

Opportunity

Teachers have long been both baffled and frustrated to find that, no matter how carefully they plan and implement a lesson, taking into account the needs, preferences, and interests of their learners, the students are likely to take away from the lesson something quite different from what the teacher planned. Despite our best intentions to help them sort out the differences between 'beautiful,' 'handsome,' and 'cute,' learners come with idiosyncratic concerns and agendas, as well as varying levels of proficiency, and once our vocabulary lesson is filtered through these academic and social concerns our students might have actually learned something about pronunciation or perhaps a new bit of gossip about a movie star (Slimani, 1992; Block, 1994).

Wait. Back up. *Our* vocabulary lesson? That is precisely the kind of thinking that can give rise to the experience I described. Rather than assuming we know what our students need and selecting particular bits of language or content to deliver to our students in hope that they will learn it, we may do much better to refocus our energies on the learning opportunities that can be created by both students and teachers (Crabbe, 2003; Allwright, 2005). Given the diversity of learners and the complexity of learning, no matter how attentive and conscientious a teacher is, she or he cannot know in advance precisely what type of language each student will need at any given moment to push forward their development. The shift from teaching to learning moves us away from expectations that students learn what teachers teach and toward a recognition of classroom interaction as a co-construction of both teachers and students (Tarone, 2006). It is now 'our' vocabulary lesson in the sense of 'teacher's and students'.' This perspective encourages us to focus on the local context and to take advantage of the learning opportunities it affords, thus making the material relevant to the learners.

This does not mean that teachers should not plan their courses, but it does suggest that plans should be flexible and somewhat open-ended, leaving space for exploration of learner-initiated topics. Teachers who work under the constraints of a preset curriculum can also take advantage of this change in perspective, and plan for multiple, recursive lessons that engage learners with required materials in a variety of ways. Viewing classroom learning as the creation of learning opportunities will likely require the 'scattershot' approach mentioned in the previous chapter (Allwright, 2006).

Conclusion

In many ways this chapter has emphasized the idea taken up in the previous one regarding the multitude of perspectives that comprise our field. It is far from a comprehensive survey, and I hope you will pursue areas of interest to you by tracking down texts that were cited, as well as looking at the recommended readings. Many of these will point you in further new directions. This is an exciting time in TESOL and applied linguistics, as perspectives on language, learning, and teaching are shifting, with new avenues being explored and integrated into existing frameworks.

Recommended reading

On language

Widdowson, H. (1993). Proper words in proper places. *ELT Journal*, 47(4): 317–29.
Widdowson, H. G. (1994). The ownership of English. *TESOL Quarterly*, 28(2): 377–89.

Slightly revised versions of both articles are also available in:

Widdowson, H. (2003). *Defining Issues in English Language Teaching*. Oxford: Oxford University Press.

Although there are many excellent texts discussing issues of language, I particularly enjoy Widdowson's treatment and his careful argumentation.

On learning

Lightbown, P. and Spada, N. (2006). *How Languages are Learned*, 3rd edition. Oxford: Oxford University Press.

This is an accessible introduction to first and second language acquisition written for teachers, with an eye toward the classroom implications of SLA theory.

VanPatten, B. and Williams, J. (2007). *Theories in Second Language Acquisition: An Introduction*. Mahwah, NJ: Lawrence Erlbaum.

This edited collection will introduce you in greater detail to the theories from this chapter, as well as several others.

On teaching

Ellis, R. (2005). Principles of instructed language learning. *System*, 33: 209–24.

Kumaravadivelu, B. (2001). Toward a postmethod pedagogy.*TESOL Quarterly*, 35(4): 537–60.

Nation, P. (2007). The four strands. *Innovation in Language Learning and Teaching*, 1(1): 2–13.

These three articles make for an interesting comparison of current postmethod pedagogical recommendations, as they rely on flexible principles, rather than attempting to outline a method.

On language, teaching, and learning

Kumaravadivelu, B. (2006). *Understanding Language Teaching*. Mahwah, NJ: Lawrence Erlbaum.

This book is a thorough and balanced discussion of the concepts introduced in this chapter.

Activities

1. Take a second look at the definitions of language at the opening of the chapter. What are the implications of each one for teaching?

2. Write down your initial thoughts on and responses to each of the main elements: language, teaching, and learning. This is a valuable document to retain in its original form and to continue to revise throughout your career. It forms the basis of a teaching philosophy, which makes your beliefs and assumptions explicit. Tracking the ways you revise the statement helps you trace your growth as a teacher.

3. Below are some sources for teacher-friendly articles based on research, help with lesson planning, and ideas for activities. Take a look through these websites for examples of particular activities. How are they explained in terms of the theories of language, learning, and teaching that underlie them? This may be explicit, but it might also be implicit and require some work to interpret:

   http://www.llas.ac.uk (Subject Centre for Languages, Linguistics, and Area Studies)

   http://www.cal.org (Center for Applied Linguistics)

   http://www.carla.umn.edu (Center for Advanced Research on Language Acquisition – a US National Language Resource Center housed at the University of Minnesota)

3
Key Concepts in TESOL

The previous chapter concentrated on the broad areas of language, learning, and teaching, and in doing so introduced you to a number of important concepts in the field. We discovered areas in which there is broad agreement, but also learned more about the wide variety of perspectives that teachers and researchers hold about L2 teaching and learning. That theme continues in this chapter, as we take a closer look at some specific concepts related to TESOL. My goal here, as always, is not to provide a definitive survey, but merely to help familiarize you with the kinds of ideas you will be learning about in hopes that this will make it easier when you do encounter them and so that you might begin to identify areas that are of particular interest to you. If you are reading this book as part of a class where you are assigned a research project (see Chapter 5 for help on conducting research) this chapter can be a source of ideas, suggesting avenues for further inquiry. Whereas in the previous chapter we dealt to a greater extent with theories of language, teaching, and learning, this chapter will lean toward the practical, emphasizing many of the issues that face teachers in the classroom.

Some of these issues have been selected because they are of particular interest to the field at present, such identities and the use of technology in language learning. Others, like motivation and culture, are those about which new students seem to be consistently curious. The chapter is roughly organized from a micro to a macro view of SLA, beginning with individual differences in learning and ending with a discussion of the ways in which larger social influences can affect what happens in the classroom. Other topics

51

include the myth of the NS, the nature of classroom discourse, the possibilities that exist for choosing and developing texts and materials, and the challenges of L2 assessment. Each item represents a factor that can influence SLA, and as such they demonstrate the complexity of the endeavors of teaching and learning additional languages.

Individual differences

One of the difficulties in developing a single, comprehensive theory of SLA lies in the fact that learning is a human endeavor, and while we can identify broad trends among large groups, individual experiences with language learning, and thus the outcomes of learning, vary extensively. Teachers know that attitudes and expectations, anxiety, personality, motivation, aptitude, age, and preferred learning styles and strategies influence language learning behavior and success. These factors interact with each other, as well as with the learning context. This is a rich area of research, and a full review of individual differences and the ways that they can affect L2 learning is beyond the scope of this text (see, however, Dörnyei, 2005), so I have selected for discussion two that are of great interest to teachers and learners, and that are often misunderstood: age and motivation.

Age

It is commonly believed that children learn language quickly and easily, and that language learning abilities decline rapidly at a certain age (often placed at around age 12), making it impossible for most adults to gain advanced proficiency in an L2. In TESOL, this is known as the Critical Period Hypothesis, or CPH (Lenneberg, 1967). Based on this belief, many countries, especially in Asia, are implementing ESL classes with very young children. What truth is there to the idea that adults cannot learn language as well as children? Most of us would agree with this, based on our own experiences or observations of adult L2 learners' speech, which is usually marked by an identifiable foreign accent and grammatical inconsistencies, especially when compared to the language of people who learned as children. Yet research on the CPH is diverse and findings are often conflicting, especially given the different ways in which the CPH has been conceived (for a concise review, see Singleton, 2005). One consistent finding is that the youngest learners are the ones who ultimately attain the highest levels of proficiency. The simplicity of this statement, however, obscures a situation that is fraught with complexity.

First, children do generally surpass adults when it comes to L2 **phonology**. The speech of children who grow up using multiple languages does have a native accent (if that is what they were exposed to). It is difficult, however, to find consensus regarding the ways in which age may constrain the development of other areas of language. The fact that many adults become highly proficient in their L2 and at least some adult learners seem to become indistinguishable from NSs (Obler, 1989) also poses a problem for a strong position on the CPH. Instead, a *sensitive* period, or multiple sensitive periods, for different aspects of language might more accurately describe the effects of age on language learning. It is crucial for teachers to recognize that advanced L2 proficiency is possible for adults and to convey this to their adult learners. Too many adults avoid the study of additional languages, assuming that developing this ability is beyond their reach.

The issue of age is also clouded by our perceptions of the ease and speed with which children learn an L2. Yet, as noted in the previous chapter, children expend years of effort acquiring language, and those abilities continue to develop even through adolescence. That governments and parents are willing to spend a great deal of money to begin teaching their children English at age four instead of at age 14 does not reflect the ease of child L2 acquisition, but rather a preference for native-like competence, a questionable goal (see the NS myth, below). This special dispensation is not afforded to older learners, however, who are often expected to reach fluency in as little as one year of L2 immersion. Many readers will be familiar, for example, with government policies mandating ESL support for migrant students for only a short period of time. In fact, many adults do make rapid gains in L2 **syntax** and **morphology** in the initial stages of learning; however, as with children, L2 development is a lengthy process. Understanding this is crucial, as this is an important area in which TESOL practitioners can take the lead in educating those outside of the field, such as parents and government officials, in hopes of influencing educational policies.

Motivation

Outcomes vary widely among L2 learners, and motivation is one factor that can at least partially explain this differential achievement. As you might expect, motivated learners are generally more successful than unmotivated learners. You might be tempted to skip the rest of this section in favor of finding a book on how to motivate language learners, but don't – that statement does not reveal the entire story (although you may eventually want to look at the suggestions provided by Dörnyei and Csizér, 1998). First, studies of motivation often run into the 'chicken or egg' problem: do learners succeed because they are highly motivated, or do they become motivated through their success? It is not often possible to determine a causal link between motivation and outcomes.

It is also difficult to define what motivation is. An early distinction was made between **integrative motivation** and **instrumental motivation** (Gardner and Lambert, 1972). The former arises from a learner's intrinsic interest in the L2, the people who speak it, and their culture; whereas the latter was seen as grounded in practical matters, such as the desire to pass a test or obtain employment. Not only are the two difficult to separate, but they have tended to be perceived as static, when in fact students may enter a class with low motivation, but later grow inspired to learn the target language. The opposite, too, can happen when highly motivated students lose interest in a dull, repetitive class. In fact, the quality of a language program and the teaching that goes on in it appear to be among the strongest motivators for students (Donitsa-Schmidt, Inbar, and Shohamy, 2004). That means that, as teachers, we shoulder a great deal of the responsibility for increasing motivation.

Arguing that conceptualizations of (and therefore research on) motivation obscure the ways that power and identity can affect L2 learners' attitudes toward the **target language** and toward learning, Norton Peirce (1995) suggested 'investment' as an alternative view. Learners will invest in language learning if they expect to gain physical and social resources (such as money or status) that will eventually help place them in the social position that they value. From this perspective, the desire to learn is seen not as a fixed, internal emotion, but as something that is shaped by the learner's experience with the language and with different speakers. This provides us with a broader lens through which to examine problems of motivation in our classrooms. Thinking in terms of investment encourages us to consider learner identities, how those might influence the desire to learn, and how and why this desire might change across and even within contexts.

Identity

Current views on identities see them as dynamic, multiple, situated, and co-constructed. In other words, with our interlocutors' help, we present different selves at different times in different contexts. In the classroom, for example, usually the most salient identities of the participants are teacher and student. Students tend to sit at desks and to ask certain types of questions of teachers. Teachers tend to stand or sit facing the class and ask different kinds of questions – often those to which they already know the answer. By engaging in these and other behaviors, both parties work together to construct these identities and others that are more specific, such as 'disorganized teacher' or 'overworked student.' At times, however, events may arise that lead the participants to construct identities that have little to do with the classroom, as individuals position themselves (or others) as snowboarders, computer experts, Kenyans, dog-lovers, parents, or feminists. Thus, from moment to moment in interaction identities are being constructed and negotiated. Those that are frequently reconstructed come to be seen as a part of who the individual 'really is,' while others remain momentary creations.

In addition to helping us understand motivation, identity has become a lens through which L2 development in general has been viewed. From this perspective, language learning becomes the '(re)construction of selves' (Pavlenko and Lantolf, 2000). Language is a primary means of constructing our identities, so a lack of L2 proficiency can be problematic not only from a purely communicative standpoint, it can also result in feelings of frustration, as speakers feel unable to show their 'true' selves when using their L2 (for accounts of this, see McKay and Wong, 1996; Siegal, 1996). Power relations that favor NSs can result in undesirable identities being imposed on L2 users who lack linguistic resources to be able to resist these positionings and construct new identities (see Harklau, 2000; Miller, 2004 for examples). If we see language and identity as mutually constitutive, the goal of language teaching then is to help learners' develop the resources with which to construct their desired L2 identities. This is often addressed through activities designed to raise learners' critical language awareness (see the more detailed discussion of this below).

Identity has also been recognized as an important part of language teacher development. Graduate school can be seen as a place where your identity changes from student to teacher, and where you discover options for the kind of teacher you hope to be. Investigations of teacher education suggest that learning to teach is less about acquiring skills and more an ongoing process of identity construction, in which personal, professional, and sociopolitical factors all play an important role in shaping the possibilities (Pavlenko, 2003; Clarke, 2008). Identity remains important in the classroom, as students and teacher co-construct identities and create a classroom culture. Duff and Uchida (1997), for example, show the complex ways in which four different teachers of English in Japan construct identities in the classroom, navigating through student expectations, administrative and curricular responsibilities, and personal politics and ideological preferences. Finally, it is important to note that language teacher identity can be particularly fragile when the teacher is an L2 user of English. More attention is being paid to promoting the advantages of being a bilingual teacher and to dislodging the belief in the superiority of NS models (see the next section), as a way of helping non-native English speaking teachers (NNESTs) develop confident professional identities (Braine, 1999; Brutt-Griffler and Samimy, 1999; for a review of NNEST issues, see Moussu and Llurda, 2008).

The native speaker myth and multicompetence

Strictly speaking, the term 'native speaker' refers to that person's relationship to the language he or she learned first. Yet, as scholars have pointed out, the phrase often takes on a whole set of connotations regarding national and ethnic affiliation, authenticity, expertise, intuition, and fluency (Rampton, 1990; V. Cook, 1999). Being a NS of English, for example, is thought by many to also entail the speaker's having white skin and citizenship in Australia, Britain, Canada, or the US. Yet by no means do these assumptions follow merely from learning that someone is a NS of English. Our globalized economy means that many people travel to foreign countries for work and education, often with families. A Korean family, for example, may move to France to work and send their children to an American school. Children raised in these families or in other multilingual environments rarely have a clear, one-to-one relationship among their linguistic, national, and ethnic affiliations; nor are their levels of proficiency usually equal in all the languages they use. The notion of authenticity is also called into question in these and other situations. Quite often the varieties of English used in former colonies, such as Singapore or India, are regarded as less 'authentic' (and thus less desirable) than the varieties spoken in Inner Circle countries (see Chapter 2), despite the fact that they are spoken natively by many. In a world in which most people who use English learned it as an additional language, the authenticity of the NS is seriously called into question. We must also recognize that just as levels of expertise, intuition, and fluency can be quite low among some NSs of a language, they can be very high among some NNSs.

Ben Rampton (1990) suggests that we instead examine individual language use and choices in terms of expertise, affiliation, and inheritance. Taking the hypothetical Korean family discussed in the previous paragraph, Korean could be described as the language of the children's language of inheritance, but it is quite possible that they may have greater expertise in English and French, as the languages they use in more contexts than Korean. The language(s) they affiliate with would be the one(s) that they felt most comfortable using, in which they felt most 'themselves.' Rampton's proposal allows us to take into account the broader social context in which languages are learned and to move away from judging L2 users' proficiency in relation to NSs or, as Vivian Cook (1999) puts it, positioning them as 'failed native speakers' (p. 195).

Vivian Cook (1991, 1992) examined a variety of research comparing the language use and cognition of monolinguals and multilinguals and concluded that the language knowledge of each group is fundamentally different. While some have posited separation of two language systems in the brain, Cook concluded that the two (or more) systems were not separate, and proposed the term **multicompetence** to describe the language knowledge of multilinguals. This perspective has provided a new, more positive self-representation for those who may have formerly claimed the identity of 'non-native speaker.' A multicompetent language user is not someone who has failed to reach NS competence, but someone whose experiences with languages have allowed her or him to develop a different set of linguistic resources. For teachers, helping students develop multi-competence (rather than NS abilities) implies a new, more realistic set of goals and models, and provides learners with an additional way to conceive of their multilingual identity (for more teaching implications, see V. Cook, 1999).

Classroom discourse

Language itself is obviously an important issue in the classroom. We have already discussed the challenges teachers face in selecting a variety of English to teach (Chapter 2). Here I would like to examine three other issues related to classroom L2 learning: the structure of classroom discourse, the use of the L1, and the question of what counts as legitimate language in the classroom.

Initiation–response–feedback

Most classroom language exhibits a number of features that are particular to that context, such as the tendency mentioned above for teachers to ask questions to which they already know the answer. Another predominant characteristic of classroom discourse is the way it is often structured around the initiation–response–feedback (IRF) sequence (Sinclair and Coulthard, 1975). Most conversational sequences work as pairs, for example, question–answer or greeting–greeting, but the three-part pattern is a common feature of classroom discourse and looks something like this:

> Teacher: (holding up a book) This is a...?
> Student: A book?
> Teacher: Yes! A book. Good.

This interactive structure was subjected to a great deal of criticism, particularly as we moved toward trying to provide classroom learners with opportunities for authentic (see more on this troublesome concept below) communication.

Indeed, it is rare in most conversation for adults to engage in the evaluation of each other's utterances in this way, but more recently the potential value of the IRF sequence has been recognized. Hossein Nassaji and Gordon Wells (2000), for example, showed how the third part of the sequence in content classes (mostly science and literature) can actually serve more as encouragement than evaluation for the students. In addition, this space can also be used to challenge the students to defend, explain, or create counter-arguments. In such cases, the IRF structure temporarily gives way to more conversational and egalitarian discourse (for an examination of IRF possibilities in the L2 classroom, see Richards, 2006). As a different way to exploit this pattern for learning purposes, J. R. Martin and David Rose (2005) advocate a conscious, structured use of the IRF format as a way of increasing access to literacy and genre awareness. They suggest using the initiation move as a means of preparing the students to respond successfully, and the feedback as a place to elaborate on responses, pointing out key textual features. Used in this way, the third move in the triadic sequence is also positively affirming, as the students have been prepared in the initial move to provide successful responses. In other contexts, Hansun Waring (2008) shows how a positive assessment of a student's response can have the unintended and negative consequence of presenting the matter under discussion as a closed case, thus discouraging further questions from students that might explore other possible responses.

The IRF pattern is one that many teachers fall into unconsciously, having been socialized into its use in their own education. As the examples discussed above demonstrate, its use is not inevitable, nor can it be categorically labeled as helpful or harmful to learning, as the effects are different across contexts. It is also worth noting that the three-part sequence discussed here is just one type of classroom discourse. Students also learn in groups or pairs, and in whole-class discussions that do not follow this pattern. All this suggests that it is important for teachers to learn about the structure and possibilities of classroom discourse, to be aware of their own language choices, and to consider whether and how they are using the IRF or other patterns of interaction to support their students' learning. The issue of what language(s) to use in the L2 classroom also falls under this umbrella.

L1 use

When I first started teaching English in Cameroon, I worked hard to ensure that my students spoke only English in class, and after two years I had become expert at using only English to explain abstract vocabulary like 'freedom' or complex grammatical constructions like the past perfect (I *had already eaten* when he arrived). Even when my students grew frustrated with being able to only speak English to me or when an English explanation took three times as long as a quick translation, because my students were learning to communicate by immersing themselves in the language it was worthwhile. Or was it?

While extensive use of the L1 is not advisable, neither is exclusive use of the L2. Studies that have closely examined the nature of L1 use during L2 tasks have shown not only that very little L1 use constitutes off-task talk, but more importantly that the L1 is used to support the L2 work. Learners working collaboratively tend to use their L1 to help each other come to an understanding of the task and their respective roles in completing it, and to help each other with constructing L2 forms (Anton and DiCamilla, 1998; Swain and Lapkin, 2000). In addition, Elsa Auerbach (1993) points out that imposition of the exclusive use of English is a political as much as a pedagogical choice, as it enforces unequal relations of power between students and teachers, denying students' prior experiences and limiting their language to childlike uses. Although it may seem like common sense to do so, forcing exclusive use of the L2 may actually impede learning (for a review, see Turnbull and Arnett, 2002).

Legitimate language

The previous section introduces the idea that some languages (such as L1s) may not be considered legitimate for use in the L2 classroom. Certain uses of the L2 are often not seen as appropriate for or facilitative of learning either. In general, the ESL classroom has favored the use of transactional discourse, that is, talk involving an exchange of information. Hence, we see activities that involve learners in ordering food in restaurants, asking for directions, or explaining and justifying an opinion. These are generally seen as 'authentic' uses of language and they are accompanied whenever possible by the use of 'authentic' materials, such as copies of menus from a predominately English-speaking country. While there is nothing inherently wrong with transactional discourse, it represents only a small portion of authentic language use. Instead, as Guy Cook (2000) points out, language is regularly used in creative ways, as well as for playful and aggressive purposes; thus our learners should have opportunities to engage with a much wider variety of language forms and functions.

While games and play have always had a place in the ESL classroom, these have tended to be used more as a diversion, and not necessarily as a means of acquisition. Yet, recent research suggests that language play may facilitate SLA. In one classroom I examined with my colleague Anne Pomerantz (Pomerantz and Bell, 2007), play was rarely sanctioned, and even when it was, both the teacher and students did not see it as a legitimate activity, but rather as a break from the serious business of learning. There was, in fact, a great deal of language play during 'serious' group discussions, but it remained covert and hidden from the teacher. Yet it was here that the most complex and varied linguistic forms were used, suggesting that students were expanding their communicative repertoires – that is, they were learning. This example, as well as other research (see Broner and Tarone, 2001; Bell, 2005; Tocalli-Beller and Swain, 2007), suggests that we should broaden our conceptions of legitimate and authentic language. Similar issues can be raised about the texts and materials used in the L2 classroom.

Materials and materials development

Complaining about textbooks is a favorite activity of ESL teachers. We can never find exactly what we want, which is unsurprising given that textbooks are made to be marketed to as wide as possible an audience. Yet even teachers who are allowed to select their own materials often use them. Textbooks lend structure to a class, making it easier for an instructor to organize a course and for the students to see the logical progression. They also make both students' and teachers' lives easier by providing a ready source of activities and reference materials in one place. Text evaluation is a local matter and any preconceived checklist will overlook local conditions. When selecting a text, it is instead wiser to begin with a broad plan and create an evaluation checklist that takes into account student, teacher, administrative, and societal needs and goals (for guidelines, see Littlejohn, 1998; Tomlinson, 2003).

Textbooks can also be overly restricting, and the readings and activities they contain may not be precisely suitable for the course or the population. It is a rare textbook that does not need to be adapted in some way. For instance, a book may contain too much explicit presentation of grammar and need to be balanced with activities that implicitly raise learners' awareness of L2 forms. Sometimes the readings are inappropriate or outdated given the students' age, interests, or culture, and outside readings must be added. In such cases it may also be feasible to use the readings, but not in the way the authors envisioned. I once taught a teacher education course where my textbook, which had been selected by the administration, advocated holistic assessment of student performance. Yet this same text gave teachers single, numerical scores on discrete skills. Rather than simply ignore this discrepancy, I used it as an opportunity to discuss with the students the differences between various types of performance evaluations and whether, when, and how each type might work for teachers or students. In addition to adapting the materials, many teachers opt to supplement a text with other readings, or even forgo it completely in favor of developing their own curriculum. Options for supplemental materials are limitless, and include brochures, advertisements, audio or video broadcasts, websites, student-created texts, and a variety of new technologies, discussed in the following section. For more on materials evaluation, adaptation, and development see Brian Tomlinson's (1998, 2003) edited collections.

The question of authenticity, discussed above in terms of classroom discourse, can also be raised with regard to materials. There are those who advocate the sole use of materials that are authentic in the sense that they have been written for a native or highly proficient L2 user audience, such as newspaper articles, train schedules, and television shows. Advocates of this approach suggest that the texts and the tasks be carefully selected to fit the learners' level of proficiency. For example, beginning-level learners might be asked to listen for one or two specific bits of information in a short clip of a television show, while more advanced students could be asked to explain and refute a certain point of view presented in the program. While many teachers are in favor of the use of such texts, others argue that a curriculum adapted or created specifically for L2 learners is more appropriate. Although some people share tales of learning to swim by themselves after having been thrown into the water, most of us were fortunate enough to have someone hold us up in the water, show us how to float and give us instruction as to how to move our arms and legs. Materials created for learning purposes may provide a similar type of support (for a survey of both perspectives, see Gilmore, 2007). Knowing the advantages and possibilities of both types of materials will allow you to make selections that are appropriate for your teaching context.

Technology and language learning

Technological developments, too, have provided numerous ways for teachers to supplement and create course materials. At the simplest level, the web offers an endless source of text, audio, and video for the L2 classroom. Even those tools that are familiar and easy for most computer users to interact with can be harnessed for innovative purposes (see, e.g., Shei, 2008, on the possibility of using the search engine Google to teach formulaic language). Texts can be enhanced to support L2 readers and encourage noticing of particular forms, by highlighting new vocabulary or structures and providing pop-up or rollover graphics, audio, video, or text that give further information. Web or computer-based writing can make it easy for learners to collaborate, revise, track changes, and get feedback from multiple sources. The internet also expands the classroom, allowing students to interact in multiple ways: through email or chat rooms, by podcasting or blogging, in multiuser domains and virtual spaces (e.g., the popular Second Life), and via videoconferencing (such as through Skype).

These changes offer exciting new possibilities for teachers in regions where the internet is widely used, but we must be careful not to assume that they will intrinsically promote L2 development. Discussions that take place in chat rooms do not automatically produce more complex student language (Abrams, 2003), and intercultural telecollaborations do not ensure that cross-cultural understanding will develop (Belz, 2003). Rather, it is *how* the technologies are used that makes the difference, thus interaction, content, language, and task design all remain important considerations. This is a rapidly changing area in TESOL, and journals such as *CALICO, Computer-Assisted Language Learning, ReCALL*, and *Language Learning and Technology* are good places to learn about the latest developments and to find reviews of software and web learning tools. (For recent reviews of the field, see Chun, 2008, as well as the 2007 issue of the *Annual Review of Applied Linguistics*, which was devoted to technology and language learning.)

Culture

As language teachers, culture is a constant underlying theme in our profession. You may be familiar with the Whorfian hypothesis, which states, in short, that the structure of language determines the way we think. Whorf's hypothesis is no longer tenable in this strong version, but we do recognize that language does at least *influence* the ways we see the world. Thus, learning a language is inextricable from learning a culture. This is an easy enough proposition for teachers to deal with if we conceive of culture in terms of food, holidays, and a few easily identifiable and simply explained customs or values. Yet as anyone who has lived in a new country knows, culture lies much deeper than this, expressing itself in subtle ways that go unrecognized until confronted by difference. Furthermore, cultures are neither static nor monolithic. As an American, it is rare that I explain a fellow American's odd (to me) behavior in terms of culture. That is, I would not be inclined to observe, 'Of course he would do that. He's American.' In such cases, we instead appeal to some trait of the individual, an implicit recognition that cultures exist along with extensive individual variation and change. And for teachers of English the problem, just as with language (see Chapter 2), becomes which culture to teach?

Teachers may extract cultural information from the local culture, the target culture, or an international culture (Cortazzi and Jin, 1999). Using materials that draw on the students' own culture may help them gain intercultural competence through analysis of their own beliefs and values. Many textbooks, however, use the second option and select a target culture from which to take this type of information. Students may find this interesting, but there is also a danger, particularly in EFL settings where students have little or no contact with members of the target culture, of leaving the students with a vastly oversimplified view of behavioral norms and values. The third option requires us to define what we mean by 'international culture.' This might be done with reference to cultures that may be familiar to the students, such as the international cultures of anime, business, or hip-hop. More generally it might entail using materials that increase students' intercultural awareness and strategies for coping with misunderstanding, thus encouraging them to gain broad intercultural competence. Claire Kramsch (1993) advocates a slightly different approach, where students critically examine both their own and the target culture, and emphasis is placed on difference, both between and within cultures. By raising learner awareness of their own and the target culture norms she hopes to help them find a 'third space,' an intercultural space.

The third space option seems particularly relevant with respect to the teaching of L2 pragmatic norms. Unlike with grammar, where certain rules of word order, for example, must be followed, pragmatic 'rules,' such as how to respond to a compliment, should instead be construed as flexible guidelines. For example, while a simple expression of appreciation is a common response to compliments among middle-class Americans, depending on the individuals and the circumstances, you might also hear reactions like 'Shut up!' or 'I'm glad you noticed' following a statement like 'I love your shirt!' These rules of use are intimately tied to identity, as noted above, and even when L2 users are familiar with NS norms, they may view them critically and thus choose not to follow them (Hinkel, 1996). This suggests that we need to present learners with options for creating that third space in which they can use language that is appropriate and also comfortable for them.

Methods for teaching culture have been shifting away from feeding learners 'facts' about the target culture or lists of phrases arranged on a continuum from more to less polite. Many teachers are opting instead to help learners explore their own and the target culture, much as anthropologists do.

Through structured observation, interviews, analysis of conversations, and reflection learners can increase their awareness of culturally specific ways of interacting and learn to identify cues to help them interpret different behaviors. Because appropriate language use can only be assessed in context, such explorations are promising for **pragmatics** as well (for ideas for developing such activities, see Riggenbach, 1999; for more on teaching culture from the perspective of English as an international language, see McKay, 2002; Holliday, 2005).

Assessment

Although the topics in each of these sections are worthy of book-length treatment, language assessment stands out more than the rest in this respect. Specialists in assessment must first define language ability (are we measuring an internal competence or should we count ability as seen by actual use?), and then decide how best to sample and measure that proficiency. Discrete point tests are one type of assessment with which many readers will be familiar. These ask students to display knowledge of a specific element of language, as is done on the grammar section of the paper-based TOEFL (for sample questions, go to www.ets.org). These tests can be criterion-referenced or norm-referenced. That is, they can be designed to see whether an individual meets particular objectives (criteria), or they can compare an individual to others who took the same test, to see where that person stands with respect to the norm or average. Tests that are designed to assess large populations, such as the TOEFL and IELTS, work hard to ensure reliability and validity, but are usually not regarded as ideal measures of proficiency. Many other options exist, such as portfolios, task-based assessments, self-assessments, and oral interviews, but these are usually considered too costly to implement on a large scale. Understanding assessment is a crucial part of language teaching because it is often a high-stakes, anxiety-inducing activity for students, and also dictates what will be taught.

Evaluation is often a high-stakes venture because it acts as a gate-keeping device. For instance, students are often evaluated for placement purposes, and a low placement may mean that they need to spend more time (and therefore more money) to reach a certain level. ESL students in primary and secondary schools that employ tracking or streaming (a practice whereby students are grouped by ability level) are disproportionately placed in lower tracks due to language difficulties, rather than by their learning ability, and/or because of poor assessment procedures that are unable to separate out the two. Too often the result is a long-term disadvantage, in that ESL students receive lower-quality instruction and are not enrolled in the types of courses that will lead them to a university education (Callahan, 2005). Other **summative assessments** are those that decide whether or not a student advances to the next level or is admitted to a particular school. In these cases, the means of assessment end up determining – or at least strongly influencing – the content of the class. Teachers are often caught between working as agents of a system they may disagree with or of upholding professional standards and teaching material that they believe will help the students learn the language, rather than simply pass the tests (Shohamy, 2005). Ethics and power play an important role in language assessment, and teachers must be aware of this and of their own role in the institutional process.

Assessment also takes place on an ongoing basis during class, and it helps the teacher see how the students are developing and in what areas they may need additional instruction or practice. Such **formative assessment** practices can also act as a check of the teaching as well as learning – if an unusually high number of students fail a test, it is likely that the prior teaching of the material, or the test itself, are to blame. It is through ongoing assessment, too, that teachers can work to counterbalance the negative effects that a poorly conceived national examination may have on student learning. Assessment done within the context of the class has the potential to be more democratic and to better serve the learning needs of the students. Teachers and learners can design and negotiate assessment instruments and goals, and work toward evaluations that are regarded by all stakeholders as fair and accurate measures of language ability (for principles of test design, specifically, see Bachman and Palmer, 1996).

Globalization and the internationalization of education have increased demand for accurate, unified instruments for assessing L2 proficiency (McNamara, 2004; for discussion of some of these new tests, see also Hudson, 2005). The very same forces that call for broad, standardized assessment, however, also force us to acknowledge the many local and international varieties of English that have developed with globalization, as well as the ways that English is used in multilingual contexts. Suresh Canagarajah (2006) suggests that rather than looking for the extent to which an individual conforms to the norms of a single variety of English (say, Standard American English), we instead seek information about the individual's complete repertoire and the ways in which it is strategically drawn on for successful communication in specific contexts. Thus, the current pull is for both broader and more local assessments. (For reviews of this complex and rapidly changing area of applied linguistics, see Alderson and Banerjee, 2001, 2002).

Societal influences on language teaching

This chapter has thus far alluded to a number of factors that may affect the activities an ESL teacher is able to do in the classroom, such as textbook choices and access to technology. Larger social, political, historical and economic forces and conditions, too, influence the work of teachers.

This becomes apparent when we compare the educational success of poor and minority populations to more affluent, dominant groups, which clearly show the negative educational effects of low socioeconomic status and racism (Ogbu, 1983; Heller, 1994; Lin, 1999; Kanno, 2008). In this section I will briefly outline several examples of the ways that social conditions can affect teaching.

With regard to immigrant and refugee populations in the US, Elsa Auerbach (1995) demonstrates how ideology and attitudes regarding these groups manifest themselves in the ESL classroom. She points out that often programs are held in less desirable or out-of-the way locations, such as small, windowless basement rooms or after hours in elementary schools, where adult students must fold themselves into cramped children's desks. The students' low status is reinforced by the content of many textbooks for newcomers, which socialize them into the role of subservient laborers. For example, students are taught polite expressions of acquiescence to use with the boss, but are not informed of ways to politely express concern about dangerous workplace conditions. On an individual level, teachers can opt to discuss these inequities with students, but the societal message still comes through in the class, informing the students of their low status in their new community.

Teacher-centered classrooms and choral repetition have been observed in many language classrooms around the world, but the causes and consequences of this type of interaction vary widely according to societal influences. In China, Martin Cortazzi and Lixian Jin (1996) note that socialization into this 'culture of learning' that emphasizes obedience and involves students in repetition of utterances modeled by the teacher, choral reading, and memorization through repetition begins early. China's one-child policy is mentioned as one contributing factor to this style of interaction, as many children have grown up rather spoiled as the only child of doting parents. Thus, teachers are faced with a class of undisciplined students who must be taught to work within a group and to take others' needs into account. Cortazzi and Jin find that far from encouraging passive, dependent learners, the teacher-centered classroom in China leads to high levels of competency, as students strive to be mentally active in class and to seek answers outside of class time, rather than ask questions in class.

A similar interactive style in KwaZulu classrooms in post-apartheid South Africa results in dismal learning outcomes and high dropout rates, yet teachers there were resistant to change involving the use of more communicative activities, as Keith Chick (1996) found. He describes the oral practices these teachers and students engage in as a type of 'safe-talk,' in which both collude to present an impression of learning taking place, while hiding the fact of low English proficiency. Chick notes that this face-saving style of interaction has its origins in apartheid, during which schools in black homelands were funded at a much lower rate than those for whites, and teachers in those areas often did not hold professional credentials and lacked training and proficiency in English. Despite efforts to close the gap, the historical legacy of segregation remains, perpetuating a cycle of school failure for KwaZulu students.

Teacher-fronted classrooms are also the norm in the portrait Canagarajah (1999) shares of Tamil students and teachers struggling with English education under the legacy of colonialism and in the midst of war. Under these conditions, resources like paper are scarce, and neither funding nor time permits teachers to create their own class materials. With no blackboards or chalk, they must instead rely on textbooks that are donated by Western agencies, and even these are scarce. Without enough texts for students, the teacher is thrust into the role of the 'knower,' limiting student interaction in favor of a teacher-fronted mode. Although students were highly motivated to learn English, a prerequisite for university admission, their resistance to these classroom practices was evident in the graffiti they added to their American-culture based textbook, as well as in their responses to in-class activities. Canagarajah understands this as resistance to linguistic imperialism, thus situating student responses within a political and historical context.

It is often difficult to separate the ways in which these macro forces create change. The interaction among history, economics, politics, and society are complex, but without a doubt they do influence what we do in the classroom. This often happens in ways we do not recognize unless we are able to step back and reflect. Developing an awareness of these issues is important for, as educators, we too have the potential to influence society.

Conclusion

In this chapter I have outlined a number of areas that must be of interest and concern for TESOL practitioners, as a way of familiarizing you with a broad array of issues, as well as helping you develop your expectations about the MA TESOL. We will turn now, in Part II, from examining the field of TESOL itself to exploring what it is like to study in an MA TESOL program.

Recommended readings

Because the subjects covered in this chapter have been quite diverse, you will best find more information about specific topics by pursuing those works that have been cited within each section. However, as an additional source for learning about the key concepts in our field you may also want to look through available handbooks:

Davies, A. and Elder, C. (2004). *The Handbook of Applied Linguistics*. Malden, MA: Blackwell.
Hinkel, E. (2005). *Handbook of Research in Second Language Teaching and Learning*. New York: Routledge.
Kaplan, R. (2002). *The Oxford Handbook of Applied Linguistics*. Oxford: Oxford University Press.

Activities

1. Individual differences such as attitudes and expectations, anxiety, personality, motivation, aptitude, age, and preferred learning styles and strategies interact with other aspects of the ESL classroom discussed in this section. How might the ways that the structure of classroom interaction, the materials used, technology, and assessment procedure influence some of these individual traits?
2. As a way of looking at the manner in which identities are co-constructed, consider how you, the reader, are positioned

throughout this book. Where do you see evidence that you are being positioned as a teacher, a colleague, or a student? How do you react to these different identities?

3. Despite the problematic nature of the construct, many schools insist upon hiring native English speakers to teach their ESL courses. Yet, L2 users of English have strengths as teachers that native English speakers who come from outside the local culture do not share. Can you think of what some of those strengths might be? (See discussion below.)

4. What kinds of interaction have been emphasized in language classes you have taken? How did you react to the different formats?

5. Find an ESL textbook to review. Look carefully at the table of contents, messages to teacher and student, and at the content of the chapters and answer the following questions:

   a. Where and with what type of learner might this text be used?
   b. How is the language presented?
   c. What roles does the text encourage for the teacher? For the learners?
   d. What types of tasks, activities, and interactional structures are encouraged?
   e. What cultures are treated in this book and how? (Note that this may be more implicit than explicit.)
   f. How is learner progress assessed?
   g. If you were to use this text, how might you do so? What would you want to change or supplement and how?

6. Go to the website of the International Language Testing Association (ILTA: http://www.iltaonline.com) and look at the code of ethics. Why do you think that this is given such a prominent place on the website? Is language testing different with regard to ethics than other types of testing?

7. While you are at the ILTA site, look in the Code of Practice at the Rights and Responsibilities of Test Takers. Think about a language test that you have taken. To what extent were these upheld by you and the test administrator?

8. Consider the context in which you expect to teach. What kinds of social, historical, economic, and political factors do you imagine influence that classroom and how?

Discussion of Question 3

According to Barbara Seidlhofer (1999; see also Medgyes, 1992) non-native English speaking teachers of English have advantages over NSs in that they can:

- provide an authentic and attainable model of L2 acquisition and use;
- anticipate areas of English language and culture that will be challenging to their students, having gone through the same process themselves;
- reinterpret current theories and materials to use them in a manner that is locally appropriate and meaningful.

Part II
Studying for your MA TESOL

4
Learning to Learn in Graduate School

As someone who is applying or has already been accepted to a graduate program, you most likely already have many years of formal schooling behind you and have proven yourself to be a successful student. Take a moment to consider your academic experiences:

- How did you learn what it means to be 'a good student'?
- How did 'being a good student' change in different contexts, say between secondary school and university?
- What kinds of academic texts have you been asked to write, and how did you learn to write them appropriately?

Some people may be able to point to a particular teacher or mentor who helped them become successful students, but for many, the answers to these questions will be vague: 'I don't know. I just learned it!' This implicit socialization is probably the norm, and while it has served many students adequately, learning through discovery is not always fast, easy, or painless, nor does it serve all students. The goal of this chapter is to share with you some of the behavioral norms and expectations you are likely to encounter as you study for your MA TESOL, and hopefully save you the frustration of trying to decipher them alone and from scratch. Note, however, that these are only guidelines: actual behavior and expectations may vary.

Let's first take a brief look at the types of assignments you may anticipate doing during your MA program. Chances are you will do a great deal of reading and writing in order to fulfill the requirements for each course you take. You might be asked to design a lesson or unit plan, write a teaching philosophy, write up an observation of another teacher, keep a reading journal, write a book review, or compile an annotated bibliography. Some of your course requirements will probably involve oral presentations. For example, you might be asked to teach a short lesson to your classmates or to lead a discussion about an article. You should also expect to work frequently in pairs or small groups. TESOL practitioners tend to value collaboration and therefore may ask you to co-author papers, as well. Your professors normally give these assignments to help you develop as a teacher and to assess that development, but also as an invitation to explore the field and learn more about specific areas you might want, or need, to know about.

I have introduced a variety of typical assignments to give you an idea of projects you might be asked to do, but in practice these are far from transparent. For example, in one class of first-year TESOL students, I asked them to write a 'reflective paper' discussing and exploring (that is, 'reflecting upon') their beliefs about language, teaching, and learning. The goal of this paper, to my mind, was to move them in the direction of a statement of their teaching philosophy, a document they would need to include in their portfolio for graduation. At the same time, another professor had also asked these students to write a 'reflective paper,' but it seemed to them that he was asking for a very different kind of text. For that assignment students were asked to 'reflect upon' specific readings for the class, discussing their impressions of an article, linking it to their own experiences, and perhaps raising questions or points of concern. This led us to discuss not only the points in common about these papers, but also the ways in which graduate students can learn about their professors' expectations and negotiate assignments.

The rest of this chapter is divided into two main sections which, I hope, will help you find ways of interpreting and negotiating assignments and classroom expectations. The first section discusses class participation and interaction with professors and peers. The second introduces the concept of academic literacy. It describes some of the challenges you may face learning to compose the academic and professional genres of the discipline in graduate school, including a discussion of the contentious and often confusing issue of plagiarism.

Interacting with professors and peers

Most TESOL professors have taught ESL themselves and try to demonstrate the same sound educational practices in their teacher education
courses that they use in their ESL classes. Because of this, depending
on your previous educational experiences, your MA TESOL course
may seem exceptionally active. Recall from Chapter 2 the discussion
of the importance of interaction in language learning, particularly
from the sociocultural perspective. Indeed, following **Lev Vygotsky**,
talking is considered to be an important aid to learning in general,
and your courses are likely to be a mix of small group discussions,
whole-class discussions, and some lectures.

In each of these formats, student participation is expected and
usually encouraged. This often includes the lecture. Most professors welcome questions and comments during their lectures and do
not perceive them as interruptions. Given the value our profession
places on the student and on interactive teaching methods, many
of us are often reluctant to lecture. I sometimes even announce
apologetically that I must 'exercise my professorial right to the floor'
when I need to lecture, a statement that acknowledges that extended
monologues by the instructor, while usual in many university classrooms, are not considered the norm here. In fact, your professors
may engage in typical lecturing behavior (that is, standing or sitting
in front of the class and talking for an extended period of time),
but they may not identify these actions as 'lecturing,' instead seeing this as a whole-class discussion. It is usually a good idea to
take notes during these (non-!) lectures, even though it is unlikely
that you will encounter many traditional examinations during your
coursework.

Group work tends to be more prevalent than lectures in MA TESOL
courses and can cover a wide variety of activities, perhaps the most
common being the group discussion. This may involve unstructured,
student-led talk about a previously assigned article, or a more structured activity in which the professor provides a topic, problem, or set
of questions to which a group must respond. The response might be
given in writing or, frequently, one member of each group is asked
to summarize their group's discussion. You may also be assigned
graded group projects, including, for example, collaboratively written
papers, presentations, or lesson plans.

Working with peers can be intimidating if you feel that they are more knowledgeable, but it also gives you a chance to try out new ideas with a small, usually sympathetic audience. Note, too, that your impression of their experience and knowledge may be mistaken. Some people quickly pick up new vocabulary and will pepper their discussion with academic terms; this does not necessarily mean that they understand them well, but perhaps that they have learned to play the academic game well! Those with a strong understanding of the terminology of the discipline should also be able to explain it, so feel free to ask your classmates for clarification. Always remember that everyone is in the program to learn, including those who have a great deal of experience. Given a difficult assigned reading it is usually equally valuable to have completed it and to join a group discussion with *questions*, rather than with the 'right' answers. Preparation, curiosity, and the ability to listen are just as important to successful participation in group work as speaking.

A final type of activity that is worth mentioning, if only because it is the one that most students dread, is the presentation. I am using this term very broadly to describe any activity where a student takes charge of the class, either to engage members in an activity or to share information. Presentations can, of course, be done in groups, as well. You could be asked, for example, to lead the class in discussion of an article everyone has read, to teach a sample lesson, or to make an informative presentation about a particular topic. In all of these instances, what your professors are most likely *not* asking you to do is to read from a prepared script. In addition, it is unlikely that they want you to repeat or provide extensive summaries of information that other members of the class have already seen.

What professors *are* probably looking for is evidence that you have read and understood the course materials and are beginning to see how they fit into the larger picture of TESOL theory and pedagogy. They want you to show this through your own response to and critique of the texts and concepts. For new MA students, and particularly for the many students who go abroad and receive their MA degrees under an educational system that is largely unfamiliar to them, the task of responding to experts' texts with anything other than agreement is daunting. For those with very little background in the field of language teaching and learning, such as someone whose undergraduate degree is in business, the task seems quite nearly impossible – and maybe even a bit unfair. How can I critique these ideas when this one article is all I have read on this topic? At the other end of the spectrum are those students who, well familiar with the practice of critiquing texts, approach each reading ready to find something wrong with it. For these students it is important to remember that publications are carefully vetted, and it is rare that an article with no redeeming value will make it into print, and even less likely that it would be assigned by your professor!

In fact, your instructors do not expect you to make a completely novel contribution to the discipline, especially in your first semester; they simply want to help you learn to evaluate research and arguments, as after graduation you will need to continue to stay abreast of developments in your field by reading professional journals. You can demonstrate that you are able to do this by identifying and examining an author's assumptions, which are often implicit even in research articles. For example, given the information in Chapter 2, you should now be able to recognize when a scholar is drawing on, say, the interaction hypothesis in their development of a particular learning activity and discuss how the activity follows appropriately (or not) from the hypothesis. Connecting a current reading to your personal experiences and discussing how the reading helps you understand those experiences in new ways is also a tactic for showing that you have read carefully. In addition, you can connect an assigned reading to other articles in the field, comparing the way different scholars treat a particular theme. Asking questions is yet another good way to help others think more deeply about a text. These can include aspects of the reading that you found particularly difficult, and in fact, identifying your own (perceived) lack of understanding shows careful reading and helps your professors see areas in which the class might need extra support.

Relationships with professors

Although many students find it intimidating to approach their professors one-on-one, it can be very beneficial for your education and your future career to do so. Visiting professors during their office hours is an ideal way to build relationships with them, as class meetings do not always offer enough time for individual attention. As you enter the job market or continue on to a PhD, you will likely need to have recommendations from one or two of your instructors, and they will be able to write a much richer letter if they know you a bit outside of class. Of course, this does not necessarily mean that you should stop by as your first visit simply to chat about a great restaurant you found. So, what are some reasons students might meet with a professor outside of class?

Early in your program you may have questions about assignments or readings. Office hours are a good time to address questions that you have about these that do not seem to be of interest to the class as a whole. Imagine, for example, that you have read an article for another class and you wonder whether it is appropriate to use texts assigned in other courses in an assignment for this class. The answer to this question will be short and it might benefit many students, so it is probably a good one to ask during class time. On the other hand, if you are wondering whether research methodology used by the author of that article would also be of use to you in the individual project you have designed for this course, it may be better to speak one-on-one with the professor about this. Of course, it is not always easy to distinguish whether a question is individual or will be of interest to the class, so you can always ask and let the professor know that you will be happy to talk later if the question would be better addressed on an individual level.

As you move further through your program you may want to speak to your professors about whether you might be able to assist them with research projects, an especially valuable experience if you plan to pursue a doctoral degree later. You will also begin to participate in the field more broadly, and your professors can act as resources to help you learn about attending and presenting at conferences and workshops. When you are looking toward completion of the MA, you may want to seek advice about continuing your graduate education or ideas for career options. You might, for example, want to find a site where you can do a teaching practicum before graduation. Professors who already have some understanding of your interests will be better able to advise you on your choices.

Relationships with peers

The people attending graduate school with you can be at least as much help during and after school as your professors. Many students benefit from working together in study groups, traveling to and presenting at conferences together, or simply in sharing information about the graduate program. Peers, especially those who are several semesters ahead of you in your program, can be a great source of information about courses and professors. Separating accurate, useful information from mere gossip can be difficult, but it is worth trying to learn about the expectations that will likely be placed upon you in the various courses you will take. For example, your fellow students can help you determine the appropriate parameters for assignments such as those discussed above. Someone who has previously taken a class you are in can tell you that your otherwise easy-going professor uses a stopwatch to time student presentations down to the second, or that the very quiet and modest Professor Jones has strong connections with the local elementary school and has helped several students set up internships there. Finally, after graduation, many of your classmates will remain significant professional contacts with whom you can find job prospects, share teaching experiences, and engage in continuing professional development activities. From this discussion of classroom interactions, we turn now to examine the interactions you will have with written texts.

Academic literacy

To begin, take a moment to examine the following samples of writing:

– do laundry
– read chapter 7
– call Maya
– go to bank
– buy batteries

cheese
4 apples
pasta
peanut butter
curry powder

You are probably familiar with hundreds of types of writing and easily identified the above two as 'lists.' How did you know this? You probably recognized them by their vertical structure – in English, lists are usually written from the top of a page to the bottom, rather than across. They also contain very little grammatical information, such as articles. You may have further recognized that these are two different types of list. The one on the left is a 'to-do' list, which is evident from the imperative verbs that begin each item, whereas the one on the right is likely to be a shopping list. Note, too, that there is some variation between the two. While one list uses a type of bullet point (–) to mark each item, the other does not. We could also create different versions of these lists, for example by numbering the items to indicate importance or the order in which they should be completed or where they are to be found in the store. In each case, however, enough of the features would remain for a reader to recognize these as lists. A list is a type of writing that follows conventional patterns that make it identifiable as a **genre** (for a helpful overview, see Johns, 2008).

Other types of writing also follow generic formats: consider newspaper articles, emails, obituaries, graffiti, or social networking websites, such as Facebook. Although there can be a considerable degree of creativity within each genre or type of text, they all follow some conventional patterns. Once you become familiar with these generic conventions, the predictable style and organization make it easy to read and find information quickly. Examples of academic genres in TESOL that you will become familiar with include research papers, book reviews, abstracts, dissertations, teaching philosophies, bibliographies, literature reviews, and reflective journal entries. Reading and writing in graduate school involve a different set of conventions and expectations than much of the writing you probably did as an undergraduate. This is because you are now becoming a specialist, and with specialization comes specific ways of constructing and interacting with texts.

Not all approaches to literacy recognize that it is situated in this way. Lea and Street (1998; see also Gee, 1996) describe three approaches to literacy. A traditional view is that literacy is a skill that, once acquired, can be used relatively unproblematically across contexts. This perspective, which clearly draws on Sfard's (1998) acquisition metaphor (see Chapter 2), is quite common and can be the source of much frustration for graduate students, whose feelings may be summed up nicely in the title of Mary Lea's (1994) paper discussing mature adult undergraduates' encounters with writing in higher education: 'I thought I could write until I came here.' Many students do not expect graduate level writing to pose problems either because they enjoy writing in general or were successful writers as undergraduates. We believe our skill in writing in past contexts will continue to serve us well. Yet, writing as an MA TESOL student or an ESL educator is different from writing as a friend, a parent, or an undergraduate. It means seeing the world in a particular way, valuing certain types of evidence, and constructing a specific textual identity. Writing is a social practice and as such is not the same in all situations. Recognizing this may help you avoid those feelings of frustration and understand why you might be struggling with writing in your MA program.

The second view of literacy described by Lea and Street (1998) recognizes that learning to write in different contexts is akin to learning to contend with a new culture. From this perspective, students need to be socialized into the conventions of the community by raising their awareness of the features of the genres that are typical in the discipline, similarly to how we described what makes a 'list,' above. Novice writers may learn strategies for constructing particular rhetorical moves, such as presenting information, contesting a point, or evaluating a claim in recognizable ways. Research suggests that student writing improves when these features are made explicit (Johns, 1995; Turner and Bitchener, 2006; Cheng, 2008), making an academic socialization perspective quite valuable. Genre analysis is often used in teaching writing in ESP/EAP contexts (Swales, 1990; Paltridge, 2001; Bhatia, 2004; Hyland, 2004).

Lea and Street (1998) caution us, however, that the socialization approach can tend to portray academic writing as homogeneous and to assume that instruction in the features of academic writing and strategies for approaching these tasks will suffice in making better writers. They advocate instead an academic literacies approach, which recognizes that writing conventions are not neutral but ideological, and that they play an important, if largely unacknowledged role in shaping what counts as legitimate knowledge. Most articles that report research, for instance, follow the basic structure of an introduction, literature review, explanation of the research methods, presentation of the results, and discussion of the results. Within this framework, certain choices are favored at the sentence level, such as the use of passive voice ('the data were analyzed'), formal language (usually words with Greek and Latin roots), and lack of direct reference to the author (most of us have been admonished at some point to avoid 'I' in formal writing). Together, these conventions, along with many others, allow for those familiar with the genre to recognize it as a legitimate contribution and to easily locate information within it. At the same time, those very same conventions simplify and obscure the complexity and messiness of the research process, the researcher, and the participants (for a full discussion, see Canagarajah, 1996). TESOL has been more welcoming than some other disciplines of alternative forms of knowledge representation, but still, the strict guidelines for presentation put forth by many publishers effectively limit contributions from those whose writing does not follow the dominant (specifically, Western) academic model.

An academic literacies perspective also highlights the ways in which identity and power shape us as writers. When I went away to graduate school my father left me with a word of warning: 'Don't let graduate school ruin your writing.' I heard this as a caution against acquiring a style of writing that involved never-ending sentences, laden with technical jargon; a style that restricted access to the ideas being discussed, as it would be largely incomprehensible to anyone without a PhD. His advice was fair enough, but how was I to show my professors that I 'belonged to the club,' as James Gee often describes academic literacy (e.g. 1996), without using some of that type of language? Would I get good grades if I wrote in 'my own' style? Today, my father would certainly pronounce most of my publications to be examples of 'ruined' writing, as that academic style has become one of 'my own' styles. Yet, as I continue along my career path the possibilities of what I can say and how I can say it expand. I now feel like a member of the club and so do not always need to prove this through my use of the most academic-sounding options and I find myself able to play a bit with the conventions. My textual identities change with the power imbued in my different social positions, thus my writing as a professor is different from my writing as a graduate student.

In my view, while we should pay attention to the ways in which generic conventions constrain the presentation of our ideas and our textual selves, we also need to recognize the ways that they facilitate the dissemination of those ideas with others in our field. Much of the technical vocabulary we share, for example, functions as shorthand for ideas that would take several sentences to describe to an outsider (consider reactions to the use of the term 'NS myth' in an everyday conversation). The predictable (to insiders!) structure of TESOL genres allows us to quickly find information. The trick is to find styles of writing that allow you to achieve your communicative goals (and get good grades) in a manner that still makes you feel comfortable with the way you as the author are portrayed, while remaining aware of the assumptions about knowledge and identity that are part of your text.

In order to gain confidence with the textual forms used in TESOL, you should quickly become accustomed to sharing your writing. This will not only make your writing stronger, but it is also a common practice in our discipline. Your professors should help you understand their expectations for assignments and they may be able to suggest ways of organizing your ideas. Peers, too, are often willing to read and comment on drafts, and share strategies for approaching different assignments. Many universities have writing centers, where peer tutors are available to comment on writing. These are often undergraduate students who may be unfamiliar with the requirements of graduate-level writing in specific areas; however, it is worth checking into as it offers another venue for talking about writing. In addition, it is becoming more common for writing centers to offer specialized help for graduate students and for L2 users.

In addition, when you read, pay attention to the ways that different genres are constructed. You can find examples of specific text types from your peers or professors online, or by using published pieces as models in creating your own texts. In fact, this is exactly what I did when writing this book. The organization of the chapters was clear to me, but I wasn't sure how to start and finish the text. Did I need to devote an entire chapter to the introduction and conclusion? I looked at a few books written by scholars whose writing I admire and found that a short preface and conclusion would suffice, without giving them full chapter status.

Textual borrowing practices

This last suggestion raises a potentially confusing and contentious issue: What constitutes 'too much' borrowing of another text? If I can borrow the structure of the article, can I borrow the structure of a paragraph? Of a sentence? Can I borrow one or two words? This can be challenging to determine for students who were raised within Western academic culture, but for those who have come from abroad to study, the specter of plagiarism can be just that – a specter; something looming and ever-present, but ill-defined. Of course, universities work hard to ensure that it is not so, providing what they hope are clear and helpful definitions of plagiarism, such as this one from my university (http://www.conduct.wsu. edu/default.asp?PageID=338):

> Presenting the information, ideas, or phrasing of another person as the student's own work without proper acknowledgement of the source.... The term 'plagiarism' includes, but is not limited to, the use, by paraphrase or direct quotation, of the published or unpublished work of another person without full and clear acknowledgment.

After reading this, my ESL students usually tell me they understand the definition, but they are less certain of their ability to avoid plagiarism as they construct their own texts. What constitutes 'proper acknowledgement' of a source? What kinds of information need to be cited? When is something paraphrased well, that is; when has it been changed 'enough'?

The usual response is that ideas and assertions that are 'common knowledge' do not need to be quoted or cited, while all ideas or words that you 'got from others' should either be quoted and cited, or 'put into your own words' and cited. The problem is, what constitutes 'common knowledge' and what exactly are 'our own words'? This oft-quoted excerpt from the work of Russian literary critic Mikhail Bakhtin suggests where some of the confusion may arise:

> The word in language is half someone else's. It becomes 'one's own' only when the speaker populates it with his own intention, his own accent, when he appropriates the word, adapting it to his own semantic and expressive intention. Prior to this moment of appropriation, the word does not exist in a neutral and impersonal language (it is not, after all, out of a dictionary that the speaker gets his words!), but rather it exists in other people's contexts, serving other people's intentions: it is from there that one must take the word, and make it one's own.
>
> (1981, pp. 293–4)

In other words, we learn to use words by hearing others use them. It is only then that we can begin to use them in ways that are particular to us, and even then, they retain traces of their prior use. They are never fully ours, and indeed if they were, lacking a history of use, they would be incomprehensible to others! What can be considered 'common knowledge' and 'one's own' are constantly shifting.

Let's take **communicative competence** as an example. When I started graduate school, each time I needed to mention this concept I dutifully placed it within quotation marks and cited **Dell Hymes**: developing 'communicative competence' (Hymes, 1972) is important for students. The words were clearly not my own and I marked them as such. As I started to feel more a part of the field, I eliminated the quotation marks, retaining only the citation to acknowledge Hymes. Now, I had partially appropriated the words. At some point, feeling the confidence of an insider, I largely ceased to cite Hymes, unless I was discussing the origins of the term, or comparing the ways different scholars have conceptualized it (as in Chapter 1). The words and the concept have become mine and part of a base of common knowledge I share with other TESOL professionals.

This process, however, is not simple. Pennycook (1996) describes the tensions that exist for students who must write with an identifiable academic voice, but at the same time avoid too close an imitation of that voice, lest they be accused of plagiarism. His description of the dilemma faced by (L2) undergraduates is also apt for graduate students and especially L2 graduate writers 'who, while constantly being told to be original and critical, and to write things in their "own words," are nevertheless only too aware that they are at the same time required to acquire a fixed canon of knowledge and a fixed canon of terminology to go with it' (p. 213). As discussed above, showing that you are part of the profession requires writing certain things in a certain way, yet following others' words *too* closely will be seen as inappropriate borrowing, thus a balancing act is necessary.

Learning to integrate texts appropriately can pose a much greater challenge to many international students who may have had little experience writing extended papers that require them to integrate texts, or those who were socialized into very different textual borrowing practices. Pennycook (1996) shows how ideas of textual ownership are culturally and historically variable, and argues for a more nuanced view of the practices involved. While discussions such as this one may prepare you to better understand *why* you struggle with integrating texts appropriately, the contradictions remain and must be dealt with in practice. It is the responsibility of both students and professors to be aware of the functions and challenges of textual borrowing.

In general, it is often a good idea to quote something when the author has done a particularly good job in articulating the idea, or when the words used are special or idiosyncratic. Of course, many student writers will feel that they cannot restate a professional writer's words more clearly, and L2 writers in particular can have a difficult time in determining what is worth quoting, what is technical terminology, and what is commonplace language. Extensive reading and experience help with both of these issues over time. In addition, remember that scholars become deeply immersed in the discourse of their profession and their writing can often benefit from being 'translated' into terms that will be understood more broadly. Doing so also helps your professor see how you are interacting with the course materials and adjust his or her teaching accordingly.

Initially, citations feel for students like a way of showing that they have done their research, and indeed, they do serve this function. However, they also express gratitude for the author's work and the way that it influenced the writer's own thinking. In addition, the way you use citations establishes your own presence as a writer. Despite my attempt to provide a fair and broad view of the field, experienced readers of this text can likely discern my personal scholarly bent through the citations I have selected and how I discuss them. One of the most important uses of citations, however, is also one of the most difficult for students to employ in their own writing. That is the use of citations to construct an argument or make a point.

Sometimes in academic texts, for example, a single statement is followed by numerous citations. This is one way that a writer can assert that a particular idea is widely accepted and not in need of discussion. The point is being assumed in that article. On a larger scale, consider what is known as the literature review. The name is misleading, because it implies a comprehensive survey of the topic at hand. Students who conceive of it in this way, however, run the risk of writing a literature review that consists of a series of paragraphs, each summarizing a particular research project or article. While such an overview is often helpful, a literature review is usually more selective and critical, examining the sometimes subtle differences between the scholars' perspectives. The review normally leads to identification of a 'research gap': while X and Y have received extensive attention from scholars, Z has been neglected. Or: while this topic has been examined from perspectives A and B, the more current perspective, C, has yet to be applied to this problem. The citations that are provided lend support to these statements. Although it may take some time before you are at ease with the common genres of the field, awareness of the ways that features of those academic texts pattern and how they function will at least facilitate your learning process.

Conclusion

You are likely to begin your graduate program as part of a cohort, moving along much the same path together during your coursework. Even so, there will certainly be students in your classes who are at later points in their education. When you are a new student, the ways they talk and behave can be intimidating, as they seem much more knowledgeable than you. Yet in a short while you, too, will be one of them. The change will be gradual, and you may struggle to adapt, as the academic strategies that made you a successful undergraduate may not always work for you at the graduate level. In the end, however, after having immersed yourself in reading, writing, and talking TESOL, your language use will reflect your changing self. Your graduate program can be viewed as a kind of apprenticeship, during which you move from identifying mainly as a student, relying on the support of experts in the field, to developing an identity as an independent TESOL professional.

Recommended readings

I suggest the following readings as they may be of interest on two levels. First, they focus on the experiences of L2 graduate students who are adapting to oral and literate academic practices in English. These descriptions should appeal to you as an ESL instructor. Second, although written about ESL students, all graduate students are likely to find that these descriptions help them to make sense of what they are experiencing and to develop strategies for coping with the demands of graduate coursework.

On classroom participation

Morita, N. (2000). Discourse socialization through oral classroom activities in a TESL graduate program. *TESOL Quarterly*, 34, 279–310.

On academic literacy experiences

Casanave, C. P. (2002). *Writing Games: Multicultural Case Studies of Academic Literacy Practices in Higher Education*. Mahwah, NJ: Lawrence Erlbaum.

See especially chapter 3, which describes the experiences of MA TESOL students.

Casanave, C. P. and Li, X. (eds.) (2008). *Learning the Literacy Practices of Graduate School: Insiders' Reflections on Academic Enculturation*. Ann Arbor, MI: University of Michigan Press.

On specific academic genres

Hood, S. (2008). Summary writing in academic contexts: Implicating meaning in processes of change. *Linguistics and Education*, 19, 351–65.

Swales, J. and Lindemann, S. (2002). Teaching the literature review to international graduate students. In A. Burns (ed.), *Genre in the Classroom: Multiple Perspectives* (pp. 105–19). Mahwah, NJ: Lawrence Erlbaum.

For information and activities for developing academic writing

Swales, J. and Feak, C. (2004). *Academic Writing for Graduate Students: Essential Tasks and Skills*, 2nd edition. Ann Arbor, MI: University of Michigan Press.

On textual borrowing

Barks, D. and Watts, P. (2001). Textual borrowing strategies for graduate-level ESL writers. In D. Belcher and A. Hirvela (eds.) *Linking Literacies: Perspectives on L2 Reading-Writing Connections* (pp. 246–67). Ann Arbor, MI: The University of Michigan Press.

Pennycook, A. (1996). Borrowing others' words: text, ownership, memory, and plagiarism. *TESOL Quarterly*, 30(2): 201–30.

Activities

1. Consider the writing style of this text – to what extent is it 'academic'? What features does it have that would you expect to find in, for example, a research paper? What are some features that you do not think of as typical academic writing?
2. Take a look back at the section in Chapter 2 where I outlined four theories of SLA and examine the ways I used citations in each. Which perspectives do you think I am more familiar and comfortable with? (Discussion below.)
3. Read Pennycook's (1996) article on textual borrowing. Then, compare each of the following statements to Pennycook's text and decide whether or not his text has been appropriately integrated, through quoting or paraphrasing, or not. (Discussion below.)

   a. Pennycook (1996) describes the 'moral outrage' (p. 214) of teachers' responses to texts they perceive as plagiarized.
   b. It is important to note that even if definite lines once existed between original and borrowed texts, these have started to blur in this new age of electronic texts (p. 212).
   c. Plagiarism is a major threat to academic life. Pennycook (1996) points out that it, 'in a number of ways, undermines the authority of both teacher and text' (p. 214).
   d. As Pennycook explains, the cult of originality in authorship is not the only Western perspective on textual borrowing. Some famous Western authors have also taken part in liberal and unacknowledged borrowing from each other's work (p. 212).
   e. The topic of plagiarism is 'muddled by moral confusion, apprehension, and general loathing' (Pennycook, 1996, p. 214).
   f. Pennycook suspects that traditional conceptions of textual borrowing may be changing, and that the highly emotional responses of some writing teachers could be viewed as a desperate rearguard attack on these new ways of writing (pp. 214–15).

Discussion of Activity 2

If you thought I was least at ease when writing about emergentism you are right! This is a very new perspective for me, and while I have great enthusiasm and hope for it, I am not entirely confident about my understanding of it and worried about representing it accurately.

These fears are reflected in my use of several long quotes, where I want to ensure that the ideas are conveyed properly. In addition, note that many of the citations follow ideas that, in the other perspectives, were treated without citation at times. For example, I rely on Larsen-Freeman and Cameron (2008) to explain what learning is from this perspective, whereas my own statements (!) were largely used for the others.

Discussion of Activity 3

a. This works well as a paraphrase of Pennycook's ideas, with a partial quote. The quote seems appropriate because the words are very strong. As the author, I would want to make it clear to all fellow teachers who read this that the characterization was Pennycook's – not mine!

b. This is an example of an attempt at paraphrasing that probably does not go far enough. If you look closely, you can see that all I have really done is change a bit of the word order and substitute synonyms:

Original	Paraphrase
there once were	once existed
clearly defined lines	definite lines
between the borrowed and the original	between original and borrowed
starting to fade	started to blur
in a new era	in this new age

c. Here I've been a bit tricky. Although I have appropriately quoted and cited Pennycook, I have completely misrepresented his ideas. Certainly, he used the words I quoted, but not to support the idea that plagiarism (a concept he largely rejects) is threatening academia! The form of this borrowing may be perfect, but the use of the quote is completely inappropriate and suggests that I have not understood his article or that I was too lazy to search for the work of someone who might support my view. Better to use Pennycook fairly and explain why you disagree with him than to misrepresent him.

d. This is another attempt at paraphrasing, but better than the b. above, with one exception. I have actually used a phrase directly from Pennycook: 'cult of originality.' Simply adding quotes here will make this much clearer.

e. Another tricky one! The quote is correct, but it is from Kolich (1983) rather than Pennycook. In such cases it is best to go to the original so that you can assess the information yourself. If this is not possible, however you can cite it thus: (Kolich, 1983, cited in Pennycook, 1996).

f. This is almost a good paraphrase of the ideas that are presented there, but I am concerned about the repetition of 'desperate rear-guard,' with Pennycook's 'action' changed here to 'attack.' It would be best to simply quote that phrase, as it is memorable.

5
Research and the (Future) TESOL Instructor

A chapter devoted to research may seem unwarranted in a text designed for beginning MA students, especially if, like many students, you believe that research is the exclusive domain of doctoral students. Before we can decide whether that is the case, let's take a moment to think about what research is.

- What does the term 'research' mean to you? Who does research and why? What are the goals of research?
- What kinds of activities might you engage in when you 'do research'? What are the outcomes or products that result from 'doing research'?
- What kinds of research have you done?
- What makes a piece of research believable to you? In other words, what counts as good evidence? Is this the same for research in TESOL as it is for other areas of your life?

If you are like most people, chances are that when you consider your assumptions about research the kinds of things that come to mind are scholars working to solve Important Problems by observing and recording information and analyzing data, which may frequently require numerical calculations. The result of all this activity is probably a report written for fellow scholars in a dense style, full of jargon and statistics, and published in an academic journal. Yet, as the final question hints, you have most certainly engaged in research yourself and it may not have been academic at all.

95

Research is merely systematic inquiry that is undertaken when a person runs into a difficulty or simply becomes curious and seeks to learn more about an object, situation, or phenomenon. It may also be done in order to solve a problem, or in Dick Allwright's more positive framing, a puzzle (Allwright and Bailey, 1991; Allwright, 2003). Let's take your decision of whether or not to go to graduate school, or which particular graduate school to attend. In making these choices you most likely sought out information from a variety of sources. You probably looked online at a number of programs and requested further information from schools that looked interesting. Friends and family may have played an important role in helping you choose, as you tried to balance professional, personal, and financial considerations. You might also have sought the advice of experts, speaking with professors and current or former students of the program. Some of you may even have visited a campus for first-hand experience. You evaluated information from each of these sources differently, taking into account more seriously those that were of greater personal importance or were more credible, and finally came to a conclusion. Of course, most research raises further questions, and you have now been faced with working through the puzzles of deciding where to live and trying to find out which courses and professors will best fulfill your needs as a graduate student. You will be able to solve some of these puzzles with the same tools you used to choose a graduate school, whereas others will require different methods of finding answers.

In short, you are already familiar with research; your experience as an MA student will simply require you to extend that knowledge and those experiences to find new questions and to use particular resources for answering those questions. As discussed in the previous chapter, library research will probably be a significant component of many of your assignments. Therefore, the first goal of this chapter is to familiarize you with some of the important sources of information for MA TESOL students and share some basic ideas for accessing that information. This section will focus mainly on finding print sources. The second goal is to introduce some principles of research and discuss ways of carrying out the kinds of small-scale research projects that you might do as a student for a class project, or as a teacher to solve a puzzle in your own classroom.

Doing library research

Certainly, reports based on library research will not be the only type of scholarly work you will do in graduate school, but for most projects you will need to find background information in the library and here you will find tips on where and how to find it that should make that a bit easier. Becoming a member of any profession means gaining familiarity with the knowledge base that members hold in common (although, as we have seen, not without controversy). One way of developing familiarity with current discussions and a sense of the historical trajectory of the profession is through reading. For most questions you have in graduate school, the first place to turn to will be library and online databases in order to find out what has and is being talked about with regard to your topic.

Finding sources

The most useful database for finding research in TESOL is the Linguistics and Language Behavior Abstracts (LLBA). As the only database devoted solely to scholarly work on language, the LLBA contains information on first and second language acquisition, sociolinguistics, **phonology**, **morphology**, **syntax**, semantics and **pragmatics**. Not all the work relates specifically to language *learning*, but much of it does. This is an excellent place to find research on language learning both in and out of classrooms. The MLA International Bibliography is another very useful database for TESOL students. Produced by the Modern Language Association, it contains a great deal of literary scholarship, but also work on the acquisition, teaching, and learning of second languages. Useful information can also be found in education databases, such as the Professional Development collection, Education Abstracts, and ERIC, which is available to all for free on the web (http://www.eric.ed.gov/). Because of the interdisciplinary nature of much applied linguistic research, you may also find relevant studies in databases such as the Humanities International Index, Communication and Mass Media Complete, and others devoted to sociology and psychology. You should also search your institution's library holdings for relevant books; however, frequently books and book chapters will also be indexed in databases.

As you begin to compile a list of works that seem helpful, be sure to take note of what type of documents you have found. Books, book chapters, and journal articles will probably be the most common and most useful types of texts. However, databases also contain book reviews, which will discuss and evaluate a book. While the book itself may be helpful, the review is less likely to be directly relevant. Any database you use should identify the source so that you can decide whether or not a dissertation or a book review is the kind of text that will be of use to you. In addition, unless your research requires it, do not limit yourself to materials published in or about English. If you use another language well enough to read scholarly articles in it, feel free to do so. Note, too, that findings from other language classrooms, say, French, are usually of value to the English language instructor, as well.

One way to begin your quest for research materials is to simply type your topic in as a 'keyword,' which is the broadest type of search you can do. This will find instances of this word or phrase anywhere in a document. It may also result in thousands of hits. If this happens you will need to find ways of narrowing your search. One way to do this is by combining two or three search terms. For example, if you are interested in exploring how to *teach listening skills* to *university students*, you could try combining the italicized terms with 'and.' Here is what happened when I tried this in the MLA database:

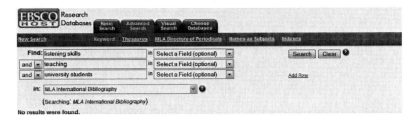

Often a search like this yields too many responses, in which case you may want to add terms. Here, however, as you can see at the bottom of the figure, my search yielded no hits. When this happens, or if the articles that come up are not at all relevant, you might come to the conclusion that no one has ever investigated your topic. This is possible, but not likely, especially if you are seeking something like ways of helping L2 students develop the listening skills required for success in a particular setting. It is actually much more likely that I will need to try again using different search terms, and in cases of too many or too few results, finding the Library of Congress Subject Headings that most closely identify your area of interest will help.

Although developed by and for the United States Library of Congress, Library of Congress Subject Headings (LCSHs) are widely used internationally (albeit with occasional small changes, for example, to accommodate concepts specific to a certain country) as a way of classifying and organizing information. The key to finding appropriate articles is to uncover the LCSHs that most closely relate to your topic. These are not always intuitive. You will find, for instance, that 'myocardial infarction' is the appropriate term to use for something that most of us would refer to as a 'heart attack.' This example suggests that having some knowledge of professional jargon is helpful in guessing what the LCSH might be for a certain concept. Using the example above, *listening skills* does not turn out to be a subject heading, although both *listening* and *listening comprehension* are. A term like *teaching methods* may work as a keyword, but if you need to narrow results and want the LCSH, you will need to use *teaching approaches*. I found this by clicking on the thesaurus, which many databases have, and browsing for the terms *listening* and *teaching*. Often you will need to try a variety of words and phrases to find precisely what works best, and there will never be only one way to search and find all relevant works. In graduate school I became interested in the use and understanding of humor by L2 users. For a long time I worked only with studies of *humor*, and missed out on a substantial and closely related body of work that fell under the LCSH *language play*.

By combining the two subject terms (*listening comprehension* and *teaching methods*), and also broadening the search to any population by eliminating the restriction to university students I had 482 results. Here are the first four:

1. Support for Foreign Language Listeners: Its Effectiveness and Limitations By Chang, Anna Ching-Shyang; RELC Journal: A Journal of Language Teaching and Research in Southeast Asia, 2007 Dec; 38 (3): 375-95. (journal article)
Find It ©W&L

2. The Impact of Vocabulary Preparation on L2 Listening Comprehension, Confidence and Strategy Use By Chang, Anna Ching-Shyang; System: An International Journal of Educational Technology and Applied Linguistics, 2007 Dec; 35 (4): 534-50. (journal article)
Find It ©W&L

3. Learning to Show You're Listening By Ward, Nigel G.; Computer Assisted Language Learning: An International Journal, 2007 Oct; 20 (4): 385-407. (journal article)
Find It ©W&L

4. EFL Listening Comprehension Strategies Used by Students at the Southern Taiwan University of Technology By Chin-Chin, Kao; Dissertation Abstracts International, Section A: The Humanities and Social Sciences, 2007 Sept; 68 (3): 978. U of South Dakota, 2006. (dissertation abstract)
Find It ©W&L

The first three are journal articles (the type of source is identified in parenthesis at the end of the citation) and the fourth is a dissertation. When you find a record of interest your library might have a button similar to the 'Find it at WSU' one that mine has. Clicking there will automatically search my library catalog for the source.

Let's take a closer look at the first citation by clicking on the title:

Title:	Support for Foreign Language Listeners: Its Effectiveness and Limitations
Author(s):	Chang, Anna Ching-Shyang; Read, John
Source:	RELC Journal: A Journal of Language Teaching and Research in Southeast Asia (RELC) 2007 Dec; 38 (3): 375-95.
Notes:	English summary.
Peer Reviewed:	Yes
ISSN:	0033-6882
General Subject Areas:	Subject Language: teaching of language; Location: Taiwan;
Subject Terms:	teaching approaches; to listening comprehension; in English language teaching
Document Information:	Publication Type: journal article Language of Publication: English Update Code: 200709 Sequence Numbers: 2007-3-11810

First, notice that if I were still searching for appropriate subject terms this record offers one more possibility, *English language teaching*, which would indeed be useful given the 482 records that were returned. We can also learn that this is a peer-reviewed article in English and that it deals with ELT in Taiwan. You can also perform searches for any of the underlined terms (note that this includes each author, as well as the journal itself) by clicking on them. Different databases can have different layouts and may present slightly different information. For example, in this view, many databases will also provide an abstract of the article. Still, each works on pretty much the same principles.

If you are having difficulty finding the appropriate subject terms, even after using the thesaurus provided by the database, the reference section of the library should also have an LCSH manual where you can look up your topic and find a list of related subject headings. I actually prefer to ask the librarians for help, as they can usually locate relevant materials in a matter of minutes. In any case, it is a good idea to experiment with the terminology for 10 or 15 minutes, but do not wait until frustration sets in to consult a reference text or librarian. Of course, if it is midnight, these options will not be available. In this situation, return to the text that first made you curious about the issue you are seeking to explore and try to locate a citation for an article on the topic. Then, search for this article in the database using the author's name and title. When you find it, check the subject terms that are listed for it and try a search using (some combination of) those. These terms are usually displayed along with the abstract and you can often click on them and perform your search directly.

This last suggestion also points to another way that you can find relevant publications – by 'mining' the reference lists of books and articles. This simply means looking closely at the reference list to identify sources used by the author that may also be of use to you. This strategy is best done with the most recent texts you can find, which will include the most up-to-date references, as well as relevant older work. There are also journals that can point you to resources. For example, the *Annual Review of Applied Linguistics* and *Language Teaching* feature abstracts of current research and state-of-the-art review articles of timely topics.

The web also offers ways to find information, and these can be a useful supplement to library sources and are crucial for those without easy access to library databases. Databases such as Science Direct (http://www.sciencedirect.com/) and Ingenta Connect (http://www.ingentaconnect.com/) are available to search for free and individual articles can then be purchased through the service. These fees can be expensive, so if you have access to a library, be sure to first check if your institution can obtain the materials for you. Also, although some of your professors may cringe as they read this, it is worth mentioning Google Scholar (http://scholar.google.com/), which can be helpful for finding a wider variety of academic sources, including both print and online articles (see below).

A final concern that some students meet with in their searches is finding only very old articles. In such instances it may be that the topic has been researched to the point of death, but speak to your professor before abandoning your plan, as it is a rare idea that cannot be revisited with new eyes for fresh insights. Another possibility is that the language used to describe what you want to study has changed. For example, although the term *motivation* is still in wide use (see, e.g., Dörnyei and Ushioda, 2009), you will also find work on the topic beginning in the 1990s that discusses this concept in terms of *investment* (e.g., Norton Peirce, 1995), as mentioned in Chapter 3. Tracing the evolution of an idea within the field to understand current trends can also be a worthwhile endeavor.

Assessing sources

Sometimes you find too much information to be incorporated into a single semester-long project and need to limit your materials. Of course, one way to do this is to focus on those that are most relevant, but even then you may have too many. Fortunately, all scholarly work is not created equal, and you can reduce your stack of books and articles by carefully evaluating them. As an initial quick tip, note that many databases will allow you to limit your searches only to 'peer-reviewed' articles like the one in the search on teaching listening, above. These are articles that have, just as the name indicates, been examined by fellow scholars, who provide feedback and suggest revisions for the author, and who also make recommendations to the editors as to whether or not the piece is worth publishing. This system is in place for many journals to help ensure a higher quality of work.

The 'mining' technique discussed above is also a good way to assess sources. By comparing the bibliographies of several books or articles on the same topic you will not only gather more sources for your own work, you will also start to see which works get cited frequently, and are thus likely to be valued and are having an ongoing influence in the field. The 'cited by' feature in Google Scholar can also be helpful in judging the impact of a particular article. Below you can see that although Harder's article has been quite helpful to me, it has only been cited 29 times since its 1980 publication (bottom left link).

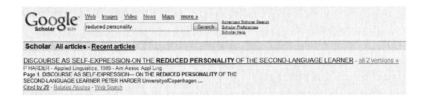

When I clicked on that link, the first article on the list was another of my favorites, 'Cross-cultural Pragmatic Failure' by Jenny Thomas. Published just three years later, in 1983, that article had been cited 631 times. Using Google Scholar in this way, as well as examining bibliographies, is especially useful in judging older studies. As you can see, Thomas's article remains quite relevant. Of course, you do not want to ignore relevant works that you find that do not get cited regularly by others (as I mentioned, Harder's article has been quite influential for me), but do carefully consider why this may be the case. Is the topic obscure and little-studied? Or is the research poorly done?

These are also questions you should ask about recent work. The aspects you should consider when evaluating the usefulness and quality of texts fall into two somewhat overlapping categories: source and information. With regard to the former, the author, type of journal, audience, and date are the types of things to examine. For example, you may not know a great deal about the author, but it is worth noting whether this person is widely published on the topic you are examining and thus can be considered an expert. You also need to examine the text type. What kinds of articles does a certain journal publish and who seems to be their intended audience? Journals such as *Language Learning, Applied Linguistics*, and *Studies in Second Language Acquisition* contain important information about SLA and are usually written by and for researchers. Journals such as *ELT* and *Essential Teacher* tend to report on research in terms of its implications for teachers. Others, such as *TESOL Quarterly* and *English for Specific Purposes*, fall somewhere in between these two. You can also, as mentioned, check to see if a journal has been peer-reviewed.

The goal and purpose of your own project will determine whether old or new work, well-known or obscure authors, or work focusing on research or pedagogy are more relevant. Imagine, for example, ways that you could use this book in a paper. Much of this text synthesizes and summarizes developments in applied linguistics, reporting on the research findings of others. This is referred to as *secondary research*, while many of the studies I have cited are examples of *primary research*, in which the authors report on a study they have done. If you were to use in your own paper my very cursory conclusions investigating most of the topics we have addressed – the Critical Period Hypothesis, focus on form, recasts, motivation – your professor would feel that you had not researched your topic very thoroughly. If, on the other hand, you were comparing the types of advice that exist for MA TESOL students as written by professors, to what recent graduates of such programs advise, this book would be a helpful and valid source, acting as data for your own primary research.

Next, the information itself needs to be assessed. This can be difficult if you are new to doing or reading research, but experience and careful reading will make it easier. First, you can examine the literature review to see if it is thorough. Do you see the names that you have begun to identify as experts in this area? You will also begin to understand the author's approach to your topic by carefully reading this section. Is the author adding to the current research by filling a gap that had not yet been studied? Or does the author take issue with previous research and suggest a different perspective or mode of inquiry, for example? Often you will see definitions of important concepts in this section. As you know, definitions of a single term in our field can vary a great deal, so you want to know whether the writer is examining your topic in a way that will be useful to you. If no definitions are given, this can be a red flag as to the quality of the research.

I also like to look closely at the research questions or, if it is not a research article, the author's goals for the article. One reason to do this is to see whether or not the questions are adequately addressed. For research articles it is worth checking to see whether the method selected for answering the questions is appropriate to the questions themselves. In other words, if you want to know how teachers plan their lessons it would make sense to ask them, but if you want to know how they actually carry out those plans in the moment-to-moment, unfolding action of the classroom, observation will tell you much more than asking. Finally, and related to your examination of the research questions, you want to check the conclusions and judge their credibility.

I would like to make one final note in this section. I have focused on print materials here; however, there is a much richer variety of sources available to use in research. You may do interviews (in person, via email, over the telephone), examine websites, or watch videos (on DVD or through the internet) to find further information. Of course, as with the print sources, the same considerations apply in judging the relevance and quality of your sources. We have been discussing library, or secondary research, but as you continue in your program and teaching, you will develop questions of your own, and find that the answers that others have suggested are not a good fit in your teaching context. In these cases you will need to be the researcher. Thus, we turn now to primary research, where you design and implement a study to solve a puzzle of your own.

Doing primary research

Not only do you need to learn to do research for your coursework, but being a teacher you are probably a curious person and the challenges of teaching will regularly raise new puzzles for you. Some questions or problems may be so persistent or pressing that they will require you to approach them systematically to find answers – that is, to engage in research. Such systematic inquiry is also necessary in making curricular changes or designing an entirely new course or program. It may even be necessary to develop a specific activity. For instance, imagine your students are interested in learning about how sounds are conveyed in writing ('ugh' as an expression of disgust) and you can find no studies of this. This would be an appropriate time to collect and examine samples of the phenomenon in order to create a lesson. This example also shows how research is something that you can engage in with your students for learning purposes, as in this case, and to solve problems in your students' lives or to improve the classroom. This type of research has been called by a number of different names, including action research (Crookes, 1993; Nunan, 1993), exploratory practice (Allwright, 1993, 2003), and frequently teacher or practitioner research. While the terms are not actually interchangeable (for some disambiguation, see Bailey, 2001), what all of these have in common is the idea of teachers tackling issues that are of concern to them and that have been raised in their daily practice – the questions arise from their daily classroom lives. Today, it is the goal of most TESOL programs to prepare their students not only to find answers to their questions in published resources, but also to do primary research. Even though you may not be teaching in your own classroom while working toward your MA, it is likely that you will still have opportunities to engage in primary research outside the classroom, in a tutoring situation, or as part of an internship.

Before delving into the basics of research, I would like to mention what has often been acknowledged as a troubled relationship in TESOL, that which exists between those who identify themselves primarily as 'teachers' and those who identify themselves primarily as 'researchers.' Traditionally, researchers have been thought of as people with PhDs who are experts in a specific area and contribute to the knowledge in that area. That is, they do research that is then used, often in a modified form, by teachers in their classrooms. The understandings that teachers have of their own classrooms have tended to be viewed as less valid than those of researchers. This arrangement, while not always the case, often has created a hierarchical division of labor, whereby certain individuals are seen as the exclusive producers of legitimate knowledge and others are restricted to acting as consumers. Despite having little or no knowledge of a particular teaching context, researchers may dictate classroom practice to teachers, who accept or ignore these mandates, according to the way they value their own understandings. While some classroom research is presented as a collaboration between the teacher and researcher, Stewart (2006) points out that even this description works to further the divide between what are incorrectly perceived as separate roles, as both groups normally engage in both activities, although teachers tend to do so with less credibility or reward. He is not alone in advocating for an equalized relationship, viewing both types of knowledge as legitimate.

Despite the changes afoot in the field and agitation for greater respect for the research done by teachers, there are numerous reasons for teachers *not* to conduct research. Lack of time or support and perceived irrelevance are certainly reasons for some, but in addition to these, a lack of knowledge of research design and implementation are challenges (Borg, 2003a, 2003b). Helping teachers develop this knowledge can allow us to take steps toward changing the culture of those institutions which do not value teachers' research, toward equalizing the relationship between practitioners and university-based researchers, and, of course, toward creating better teachers and better learning experiences for our students. With this in mind, we can now turn to our discussion of research methods.

Research ethics

I put this topic, however briefly, at the forefront of this section because, just as teachers have sometimes found themselves exploited by researchers who seek only to further their own careers, our students can be at risk for exploitation when we, as their teachers decide to conduct research in their classrooms. Research participants should be allowed to choose whether or not to participate in a project (and this raises special concerns with children and other populations who may not be able to provide **informed consent**, indicating that they understand the project, their role in it, and how the information collected will be used). There is an inherent power imbalance when one person assesses the performance of another, and you must always keep this in mind and ensure that you do not coerce your students into participating in a project that only furthers your personal agenda and provides no benefits to them. Allwright (2003) insists that the main area of concern in the language classroom should be its quality of life for all participants. This suggests that rather than doing research *on* your students, you might do it *for* them, or even better, work collaboratively to do research *with* them (Cameron et al., 1992). Undertaking research requires you to be vigilant with respect to research ethics to ensure that the project is conducted with fairness and openness.

Designing research questions

A research project starts when you become curious (or perhaps troubled) – you have a question for which you would like answers (or a problem you would like to solve). Perhaps you read an article that suggested that students will produce more and more sophisticated language in online discussions than in face-to-face classroom talk (e.g., Kern, 1995), and you wondered whether this would also be the case for your very quiet class. Or you may have encountered an unusual situation, such as a class which seems particularly resistant to completing their homework, and you want to understand why this is the case in order to come up with a solution. In either instance, in the initial stages of your inquiry, you will want to find out what others have found with regard to your puzzle. This will be done through library research, as described above. Learning about how others have approached a similar problem will help you refine your questions and make them 'researchable' so that you can design your own inquiry.

A researchable question is neither too broad, nor too specific. It should also suggest a way of answering that question, that is, a research method. In the first example, above, you can ask, 'Will my students produce more and more sophisticated language in online discussions than in face-to-face classroom talk?' This question is suitable for inquiry, but only as long as you have a clear way of defining what 'more' and 'more sophisticated' language is. For the former, will you count individual words? The number of turns each speaker takes? Length of turns? The latter case is even thornier, opening the possibility of looking for differences in vocabulary, grammar, and discourse. These are not insurmountable problems, however, and a perusal of the literature will allow you to see how other researchers have undertaken to solve them.

What do you think would be an appropriate way to state a research question regarding the homework problem? Consider some other topics, such as those below. What might be some research(able) questions you could ask about them? Look out for terms like 'better' and 'learn' and think about how you might define those within a research project.

- Providing feedback on oral language use
- Acquisition of articles – a, an, the
- Group work
- Integrating content instruction (for example, mathematics or business) with language instruction
- Teaching social functions of language (for example, greetings or invitations)
- Relationship between teachers and administrators, or teachers and parents

Choosing and implementing research methods

Once you have framed a question in such a way as to make it manageable for research, you will need to decide how to find answers. As I mentioned before, the question itself should suggest a way of answering it. Let's take another look at the question regarding students' reluctance to do their homework, which you probably phrased something like this: 'Why don't my students complete their homework?' Now, because we often think of research as complex and esoteric, we may overlook the most straightforward means of answering this question – ask them! Of course, the issue is a bit more complicated than that, as you must decide how best to ask. Will a whole-class conversation yield the richest results or will students feel more comfortable discussing the issue in small groups and then sharing the results without specifying individuals? Perhaps your students might prefer to express their thoughts in writing, either on paper or via email. You might even set up a way for them to answer this question anonymously.

Of course, sometimes asking a question directly is not helpful, as when students are reluctant to share negative reactions about a class, fearing for their grades. For some research questions it may not be feasible to ask directly because, stated in this manner, the topic will seem very abstract and removed from the lives of the people you are interested in. Let's say, for instance, that you are teaching English to a class of women who have recently immigrated to your small, rural town and you wonder about the value of English for them, particularly with respect to their gender, and how the context influences their language use. While you may receive some responses by asking 'What is the value of English for you, as an immigrant woman in this town?' the answers are likely to be lacking in concrete detail and may rely on stereotypes. As Wolfson, D'Amico-Reisner, and Huber (1983) pointed out, our intuitions about our own language use are profoundly unreliable. In such cases you might need to ask different, less direct questions to elicit stories about how the women live in this new environment, or you may need to engage in observations of their lives outside of the classroom.

The other hypothetical situation we have been discussing regarding differences in the quality and quantity of language used in online and face-to-face discussion certainly involves a research methodology that would pose a challenge for a novice researcher to design. You would have to decide when and how to collect online and face-to-face interaction, as well as how much of each to collect, carefully making sure that the two situations would be comparable. In this case, however, your task can be greatly simplified by following the procedures described in the initial study which caused you to consider how your own class might react in these two interactional contexts. In other words, you can copy, or in more academic terms *replicate*, part or all of this research. Replicating a prior study is not only a good way to learn about and practice research skills, but such work is also valuable to the profession, as we learn more about how a particular phenomenon plays out among different learners and across different learning situations (for a discussion of the importance of replication studies, as well as the different types of replication and challenges to doing such research, see Gass and Polio, 1997).

One of the most important points to remember about research methodology is that your choice of method arises from the question. Some questions will require you to observe language and behavior, while others will best be answered by talking with individuals or groups. Sometimes experiments or, more common in our field, quasi-experiments (those in which subjects are not assigned randomly to different groups) will give you the best answer. You may need to gather and examine particular documents at times. Often a combination of these methods is necessary to obtain a detailed picture of the issue of interest. This also means that sometimes you may need to employ methods that are not appealing to you. My own preference is to gather video or audio recordings of interaction for close examination; however, sometimes I become curious about phenomena that cannot be examined in this way and I must either change my questions, or take a deep breath and jump in.

- Imagine that, rather than asking *why* your students did not do their homework, you were curious about the processes they used to approach a certain homework assignment. Consider how your methods might need to change in that case, if you wanted to know *how* they did their homework.

Analyzing data

In general, data analysis is a way of finding dominant patterns in the data, as well as idiosyncratic responses, which are often as revealing as the predominant replies and may point to new avenues of inquiry. Although I have put data analysis as a separate section, quite often it really starts during data collection. As you watch people interact and listen to their answers to your interview questions, for example, you will begin to see patterns and possible responses to your research questions. You can then build on these hunches more systematically, changing your research methods as needed, for instance by asking questions that pursue closer examination of a particular theme that has arisen. Taking our hypothetical case of immigrant women's experiences with English, imagine that you hear them speak a great deal about using English in professional contexts, but very little with regard to interacting on behalf of their children in educational or medical contexts. Both the predominance of one theme and the lack of the other would suggest directions for further inquiry. Of course, in a quasi-experimental situation, such as when you are teaching a particular grammatical structure to two classes in a different way, you may resist making any changes while the project is underway. This does not mean, however, that you need necessarily resist speculation as to the outcomes of your project.

Different types of data can be analyzed in different ways, as can the same data. That sentence may seem ridiculous and maybe even meaningless, yet it does bring out an important point. What I mean is that certain types of data lend themselves to certain types of analysis. So, again, using the project with immigrant women, if you have collected richly detailed stories about these women's lives, it is unlikely that you will want to reduce their intricate narratives to a series of numbers, showing how many times they mentioned, say, their children's education (although such a number *can* confirm for you that this was a theme that was mentioned 'often,' so that you do not rely merely on your impressions of the data). Later, perhaps, you become interested in the modal verbs used by these women in telling their stories and how they change over time. Although you may want to also examine the contexts of use, in this case you may learn a great deal by counting how many times a particular modal was used and graphing the changes in its use over time.

Although true for all aspects of research, data analysis, in particular, is best learned by doing, especially with the support of a mentor. In your early stages of development as a researcher, you may want to work cooperatively on projects in order to see how others approach analysis. When doing research that is more qualitative in nature, it can be difficult to find ways to approach the data that represent it fairly and without merely summarizing. With regard to statistical analysis, the variety of tests available, each for a specific problem, can be bewildering. But do not be intimidated by this. You can always seek assistance in determining which test is appropriate for your data and interactive calculators, which also usually provide help in interpreting results, exist on the internet for many of the major tests.

Finally, it is important to anticipate that your findings may be less than satisfactory. Imagine that you are testing what you believe to be an innovative technique that will be highly effective in teaching the present perfect (I *have visited* the zoo twice already this week), but your results show that it works about as well, or even slightly worse than your usual lesson plan. While this will certainly be disappointing, results like this often spur further research questions. You can consider why your innovation was not successful, which may lead you to ways of changing it, or it may point to a completely new puzzle to solve.

Reporting data

Once you are satisfied that you have answered your original research question (which, as noted, does not always mean that you are happy with the results), it is time to consider to whom, how, and where you might disseminate your findings. If a problem was very specific, such as the lackadaisical attitude toward homework in your class, you may want to share your findings solely with your students and work together to solve the issue. Of course, other instructors at your institution are likely to have experienced this same dilemma and may also be interested in your findings. In fact, this is an issue that instructors around the globe confront. While the question of who will be interested in the results of your research will vary, despite the specificity of your teaching context, few problems are truly relevant to your class alone. At a minimum, fellow instructors in your institution are likely to be interested in your findings, and often you may want to seek an even wider audience.

If you feel it is mainly appropriate to share your results with a very local audience, you may choose to present your findings informally, in a meeting or teachers' discussion group, or in a written report that can be referred to in the future. However, as noted, quite often even issues that seem to be idiosyncratic can have broad appeal, so you should consider making your results more widely available. In such cases you can seek out conferences or publications at the local, national, or international level at which to share your work. This is also a valuable means of professional development and many of the suggestions in the next chapter discuss venues for sharing your data.

Conclusion

This chapter has provided only the briefest of overviews of research in order to give you a taste of the kinds of activities and ideas you will be likely to encounter during your MA program. It is not a substitute for a course (or two!) on research methodology. The books listed below are sources for further information on both library research and primary research. Research can also be an important part of continuing professional development, the topic of the final chapter.

Recommended readings

Perry, F. (2005). *Research in Applied Linguistics: Becoming a Discerning Consumer*, Mahwah, NJ: Lawrence Erlbaum.

This is a very thorough guide to finding, reading, and evaluating different types of research in our field. The text will be helpful both for interpreting the studies you read and for writing your own syntheses of the scholarly work of others.

Helpful guides on doing primary research

Freeman, D. (1998). *Doing Teacher Research: From Inquiry to Understanding*. Boston, MA: Heinle & Heinle.
Mackey, A. and Gass, S. (2005). *Second Language Research: Methodology and Design*. Mahwah, NJ: Lawrence Erlbaum.
Richards, K. (2003). *Qualitative Inquiry in TESOL*. New York: Palgrave Macmillan.

For more discussion on the teacher–researcher relationship this series of articles by Simon Borg is concise and available online in the publications section of the TESOL website (http://www.tesol.org/ Find the archives of TESOL Matters under 'More Serials Info.'):

Borg, S. (2002). Research in the lives of TESOL professionals. *TESOL Matters*, 13(1).
Borg, S. (2003a). Teachers' involvement in TESOL research. *TESOL Matters*, 13(2).
Borg, S. (2003b). Teachers, researchers, and research in TESOL: seeking productive relationships. *TESOL Matters*, 13(3).

Activities

1. Carefully review a journal that is of relevance to ESL practitioners to determine the preferred writing and research styles, audience and topics covered. What *types* of articles are in each issue (e.g., theoretical discussions, book reviews, teaching tips derived from

experience and/or research, short notes on research findings, announcements of interest to the audience)? What *topics* do the articles cover? Look, too, at the style of the articles. What is the structure of the articles? Do they include an abstract? What type of information is usually put in the introduction? Is there a literature review?

2. Think of a topic that interests you and make a list of words or terms that you think will help you find research materials relating to it. Try different combinations of these words in a relevant database. Which terms give you the best results (relevant articles, and neither too few nor too many hits). Select three or four articles for careful evaluation. What kinds of articles have you found (review articles, primary research, etc.)? For research articles, what are the author's research methods? What are the findings? How does the information reported in these articles make you adjust your own area of inquiry?

3. Think of a topic you would like to explore. Create one or two research questions for it. What terms will you need to define in order to do this research? What will be appropriate methods to use to answer these questions? What kinds of information will you need to collect and how will you collect it?

6
Professional Development in and beyond Graduate School

You probably already have some ideas from the last chapter about how to grow as a professional – by conducting and sharing research. In this chapter we delve into this in greater detail and make further suggestions for ways that you can begin developing as a teacher in and after graduate school. And, while searching for a job may at present seem far away, finding that ideal job will be much easier if you start preparing now. In addition, by participating in the activities described in this chapter you will become more familiar with your chosen field and find your transition from student to first-time teacher much less stressful.

'Do EFL teachers have careers?' This question served as the title of Bill Johnston's (1997) article, in which he examined the life stories of 17 EFL instructors in Poland in order to better understand their working lives and the ways in which teaching ESL might be conceptualized. The answer, as it turned out, was not 'yes' or 'no,' but varied greatly both across and even within respondents, who named different qualities for people described as 'professionals.'

- What does it mean for someone to belong to a profession, rather than a job?
- Do you consider yourself a professional – or future professional?

Sociologist Eliot Freidson (2001) characterizes professionals as individuals with specialized knowledge and skills, who are committed to their work and to the ways that they can advance the public good through it. The professional group itself defines and guides members, often through the representation of a strong professional organization which acts independently of government control to protect the profession and advance its interests. Thus, autonomy and self-regulation, in his view, are important characteristics of professionalism, both at the level of an individual's daily work and more broadly within the group as a whole. This, however, is an idealized description of what it means to be a professional; not all those who teach will consider themselves professionals according to each of these aspects, nor will all teachers use the term uniformly.

One of the valuable aspects of Johnston's (1997) article is that it not only forced us to question what we meant by 'professionalism' in TESOL, but it also illuminated the ways in which professionalism may not be uniformly desirable for members of the field. He points to, for example, the flexibility of part-time or contractual work as advantageous for some. At the same time, he emphasizes the importance of a core of professionals to sustain and advance ELT, whose practitioners often continue to experience marginalization within the wider field of education. Today, just as when that article was written, many instructors around the world still labor under less than ideal conditions, working long hours without permanent contracts. Finding full-time work is often a challenge for ESL instructors, and it is routine in many parts of the world for highly qualified non-native English speaking teachers to be paid less than native English speakers with no training or education in ELT. Thus, professional development is important on a personal level, for continued growth as a teacher, and more broadly, as a way of maintaining and strengthening the status of our discipline.

Depending on where you work, you may be expected or even required to participate in continuing professional development, but many non-governmental institutions do not require such activities by their instructors and the local professional culture will dictate whether doing so is the norm or not. In other words, in some contexts your continued growth as a teacher will be automatically facilitated, whereas in others you may have to struggle to gain the time and support necessary to do so. While the former situation is likely to be much easier, in the latter your efforts may ultimately act as a catalyst for getting others involved, thereby strengthening your institution. I will begin by discussing activities for professional development in general, and then move on to a few tips specifically about preparing for the job market.

Activities for professional growth

You will quickly notice that a theme that runs through virtually all of these activities is 'meeting people.' Indeed, as with most careers, your advancement is helped (unless you are rude and insufferable) by networking. A single, trustworthy mentor is invaluable, but no one person has all of the answers, and it is important to learn from a variety of perspectives. The more people you meet, the more ideas you will get, the more different experiences you will hear about and be able to weigh against your own, and the more opportunities you will encounter. Also, for each of the suggestions below, remember to document your participation, for example by saving letters or emails requesting or thanking you for help and keeping conference schedules that provide evidence of your presentation, as these should be added to the teaching portfolio you begin to assemble in graduate school.

Professional associations

Probably the simplest and most important step you can take first is to join and become active in professional organizations. International professional associations include IATEFL, TESOL, and AILA and there are usually similar organizations at the national and local levels. There is an annual fee for membership, which is usually much less expensive for students, as these associations provide many services for their members that all act as networking possibilities. Members are kept up-to-date on news and events with periodic newsletters. Often participation in at least one Special Interest Group is included with membership, and this group will usually also produce a newsletter. These groups often focus on teaching a specific population, such as elementary students, or a specific skill, such as pronunciation. Many organizations offer awards and scholarships to their members, for example, for travel to their annual conference or to support a research project, and quite often these are targeted specifically at graduate students as a way of supporting their growth and encouraging their involvement in the organization.

Professional organizations are also important in that they advocate for us and help us to do so as individuals. Members of TESOL, for example, work to ameliorate the status of part-time instructors through their Caucus on Part-time Employment Concerns. The association also maintains an Advocacy Action Center on their website to alert US ESL instructors of pending legislation that will affect language education and language policy. Similarly, the Australian Council of TESOL Associations (ACTA) website helps members keep up to date on topics of interest in terms of the profession and related issues, like literacy, multiculturalism, and the rights of indigenous peoples. Because of concerns surrounding the ways that language analysis was being used by governments as a way of determining the country of origin of asylum-seekers, the British Association of Applied Linguistics (BAAL) has endorsed a set of guidelines to be used when relying on a refugees' linguistic background as a way of determining national origin.

Getting involved in these associations can mean any number of things. You can:

- attend meetings
- volunteer to help with a newsletter
- lend your time to work on an advocacy campaign
- help with conference planning and organization
- register delegates at a conference
- run for an office
- edit your Special Interest Group's newsletter

As soon as other members see that you are committed to the organization, you will find that your involvement continues to grow, as others request help from you. List your memberships and any activities in which you have participated through the group on your CV. Also as documentation, you can also save any emails or certificates you receive that thank you for your service.

Student organizations

In Chapter 4 the importance of your fellow graduate students as a source of educational and emotional support at present was introduced. Here, we must note their importance in professional development, as your current peers are also your future colleagues. While you will certainly find yourself interacting as part of an informal network of friends who also discuss school and work, it can be worthwhile to join (or form, if an appropriate group does not already exist at your school) a more formal student organization. This might be a study or research network in your department, or a university-wide club for teachers of all sorts. If you are not Korean and have never been to Korea, but want to find employment there, you might see if there is a Korean Student Association on your campus, where you could meet Koreans and begin to gain familiarity with Korean cultures and customs. These organizations are places to discuss and collaborate on research projects, study texts including and beyond what has been assigned in classes, and share problems, ideas, and questions. Many such groups invite speakers to campus, and organize events, such as small conferences. These types of activities can enrich you personally and professionally, and also serve as evidence after graduation of your commitment to the field.

Getting involved online

Shy? Is all of this talk of meeting new people making you feel queasy? Then you are a perfect candidate for internet-based teacher development activities. Joining email lists and online discussion forums, often available through professional associations, is another excellent way to keep abreast of trends in the field. Novice instructors can quickly learn what topics are of current interest to others in the profession and how they are being discussed. You can also post your own questions to see what others think. Conferences, workshops, public lectures, and other opportunities are regularly announced in these forums. Email is also an excellent way to learn about new publications. In fact, you can sign up with most publishers to receive regular emails about new books and products. If there is no professional association in your area, the first step to forming one could be to establish an online community. Online interaction is particularly important for those who are working under isolated conditions, either professionally (as the only ESL instructor) or physically (in very small towns or rural locations).

Gaining experience

For those who are beginning a graduate program with little or even no teaching experience, it is very important to gain some practice before completion of the program. While most MA programs will require you to complete a practicum or internship, I mention this here to emphasize its importance and suggest ways that you might become involved beyond that particular requirement. Ideally, you will want to be responsible for teaching a class of your own, even on a volunteer basis, in order to show your ability to design and carry out lessons. However, if this is not possible, you can also gain experience through tutoring individuals or small groups. You might also look into the possibility of acting as an aide to an experienced ESL instructor, and perhaps doing supervised teaching. Keep in mind the types of learners you hope to teach in the future and try to work as much as possible with that group.

Those with extensive teaching experience may want to use graduate school as a way to explore teaching in different contexts or with different populations of learners. In addition, graduate school is also a good time to try on new roles to see how they fit. Have you always been curious about administrating an ESL program? Are you unhappy with the large-scale assessment practices of your institution? Have you not been able to find a textbook for very young ESL learners that fits your needs? In addition to adding to your teaching credentials, your time in graduate school can allow you to pursue these types of issues and broaden your expertise. For both novice and experienced MA TESOL students, activities done during graduate school should help you position yourself to obtain the kind of job you desire after graduation or to take on new responsibilities when you return to your position.

Reflective teaching

Once you are teaching, you can begin to engage in reflective teaching activities (see, e.g., Schön, 1983; Richards and Lockhart, 1996), which became popular in the 1990s as a way of encouraging teachers to seek change in their own classrooms through structured self-observation and investigation, rather than relying solely on the advice of scholars who were unfamiliar with daily life in the classroom. In addition, it was recognized that each class is a specific context; the same activity will be received differently by different classes, and even the same students will respond variably from day to day or even moment to moment. As such, reflective teaching is closely related to the practitioner research described in the previous chapter, in that it involves teachers collecting data, reflecting upon it, and implementing changes based on their findings. One main difference is that there is less emphasis on making findings public and a greater focus on engaging in these activities for professional growth, developing a better understanding of the process of teaching and, in doing so, becoming a better teacher.

Reflective teaching activities require teachers to examine their own beliefs and assumptions about learning, teaching, language, and learners. As with some of the types of research mentioned in the previous chapter, students can also be involved in many of these activities. Numerous excellent texts that suggest activities for doing this are available (see the list at the end of this chapter for recommendations) and you can work through them on your own, or by starting a reflective teaching group. Working with other instructors online is one way that some teachers have managed to create reflective teaching groups that fit everyone's busy schedule.

Conferences and workshops

Conferences and workshops are where you will find the most cutting-edge work in the field being shared. Published accounts of research findings can often take years to find their way into print, but most are first shared publicly in these venues. Although presenting at a conference is an admirable goal, those who have never been to one can first simply attend in order to become familiar with the various activities. Not only will you hear reports of recent research, but you can also learn about new publications at the book exhibit and meet your colleagues at social events. You can begin by attending a local conference and work your way up to presenting at an international one.

When you are ready to present at a conference try to find samples of successful submissions to use as models (see two in the activities section at the end of this chapter). The conference proposal is a genre with its own specific conventions and you will have a greater chance of success if you follow those. A professor or classmate might be willing to share an example, and sometimes the association hosting the conference will provide one, in addition to their more general guidelines. You usually also need to submit a very short description of your proposed session, and plenty of these can be found in prior conference proceedings posted on the website. You will also need to choose the type of presentation you are going to make, usually either a paper or poster. Many first-time presenters prefer to share their findings through a poster. This allows them to avoid the formal presentation, which can be intimidating, and also has the advantage of being able to engage in prolonged, one-on-one interaction while the poster is being displayed. Do not be discouraged if your submission is rejected. Some conferences must reject 50 percent or more of the submissions they receive, although smaller, more local venues are likely to have a higher acceptance rate.

When your first proposal is accepted, carefully prepare your presentation. If you are presenting a paper, you will want to read the information for presenters to find out whether or not rooms will be equipped with PowerPoint and whether handouts are encouraged or discouraged (due to environmental concerns, many meetings are now trying to cut down on paper consumption). Make sure you practice your presentation so that you are confident in its completeness and certain that you can stay within the time limit. Note that by 'practice' I mean 'say out loud.' Silent reading will not allow you to identify gaps or awkward wording in your presentation, nor will it prepare you adequately for the actual delivery. Audio- or videotaping a rehearsal of your presentation can also help you avoid the kind of embarrassing slips that result from lack of proper preparation, as well as check your timing and adjust your body language, if needed.

Remember, too, that you are speaking to your peers, and can assume that they share a great deal of the same specialized background knowledge as you. Thus, they want to hear more about how you have worked with a certain problem, rather than how others have. In other words, spend plenty of time on your findings, rather than on the background. When presenting a poster, be sure that you use a font that is large enough to see from a short distance away and that you make it easy for the reader to follow the order of the information. Also, although you will remain with your poster for some of the time, and thus be available for questions, people may come by when you are not required to be present, so be sure to make the information as complete as possible and have your contact information available.

Publishing

When your presentation has been warmly received you may want to consider expanding it into a publishable paper. (This is also the time to make any changes to it based on feedback you received when presenting.) Note, however, that your first publication does not have to be a ground-breaking article in the *ELT Journal*. Remember the association newsletters mentioned above? These are excellent spaces for first publications. Publishing in smaller venues allows you to report more informally on research or simply share a teaching tip, rather than try to write up a lengthy, formal paper. Book reviews are also excellent first publications and offer a valuable service to the profession. It is also not too early in graduate school to begin saving your innovative lesson plans – you may eventually want to make them into a textbook. Finally, the web offers myriad ways to publish your ideas electronically and receive rapid feedback. An excellent and very readable source for learning about the publishing world is Casanave and Vandrick's (2003) edited collection. In this volume new, experienced, and non-mainstream writers share the challenges involved in getting a text published, and how they negotiated these.

Preparing for the job market

All of the activities described above will certainly improve your employment prospects, as they will help you stay informed and also demonstrate your commitment to your profession. There are other things, too, that you can do during your short time in graduate school to prepare yourself for the job market, the first of which is research what jobs are available. You should become familiar with the postings early on in order to see what kinds of positions open up in different parts of the world, and what salaries and benefits are typically offered for different positions and teaching loads. The websites of professional organizations often post job offers from around to world and these are usually from large, reputable institutions. You can also find jobs at the thousands of small, private schools around the world by going to sites such as Dave's ESL Café (http://www.eslcafe.com/), which has been a trusted site for ESL information since the early days of the web. This site also has numerous discussion forums. The similarly named David's English Teaching World (http://www.eltworld.net/forums/) is a more recent addition, which also has extensive forums for sharing information about working conditions around the globe.

Careful reading of the information on these forums is important. These are good places to start, but do gather information widely and evaluate it with a critical eye. It can be difficult to tell whether the negative posting about a school from one person accurately reflects that institution's working conditions, or whether that person was merely a disgruntled employee. You might check for other postings by the same person to try to assess this. You can also assess the institution on whether or not it requires some kind of degree or certification for its instructors, and how many contact hours are considered full time. Contact hours refers to your actual time in the classroom, and in professional institutions that expect their instructors to prepare properly for each class and provide their students with feedback, 20 contact hours is full-time. In the end, it is always best to try to obtain information from people you trust who are familiar with your situation and with the teaching institution to which you want to apply.

Also while in school you can begin to research and prepare the certifications or documentation that will be necessary for your job. This is certainly true if you plan to teach in a country where you grew up and feel you are quite familiar with the social customs, but even more so if you want to teach in a country that you have only experienced, say, as a tourist. What do application materials look like in different countries? Should you include a picture of yourself or not? How much of your education should you include? High school? Elementary school? Should you mention your past employment or education that was not directly related to teaching ESL? Unfortunately, as mentioned previously, non-native English speaking instructors should be prepared to defend their proficiency and credentials on the job market. Always present your multilingualism as an asset, emphasizing your intercultural awareness, your appropriateness as a model for your students, and the ways that your knowledge of their native language(s) will make you more responsive to their needs. This preparation should be done in conjunction with your perusal of the job announcements so that you can easily have on hand the appropriate documentation when you are actually ready to apply for a job.

In addition to maintaining a paper portfolio, you may want to consider creating and maintaining an e-portfolio through Google sites, for example. A portfolio (paper or electronic) can provide evidence of your professional abilities and burgeoning leadership in the field. You can include syllabi and lesson plans, video recordings of your teaching, research reports, your teaching philosophy, and evidence of professional development in the form of conference presentations and publications. It is also helpful to have peers and supervisors observe your teaching and include their written report in your portfolio.

If your university maintains a career services center, take advantage of it. These centers offer help in identifying appropriate positions, but more importantly they often have sample job correspondence you can look at. They can also evaluate your CV and cover letters to help you make them stronger and tailor them for different contexts. The staff may allow you to do a mock interview and give you feedback on how better to represent yourself. This can give you an idea of the types of questions that will be asked, and allow you to practice talking about your teaching philosophy and your strengths and weaknesses (or, framed more palatably, 'areas in which you are striving for improvement'). If these options are not available to you, seek out a supervisor or more experienced peer to help you.

As a final note, I strongly suggest that you keep a journal during graduate school. On a personal level, documenting both your social and educational experiences will help you remember this time in your life and chart the changes you went through. On a professional level, such a diary will provide you with endless questions to explore throughout your career. While in school it is difficult enough to complete required readings and assignments, let alone follow up on all of the interesting books and articles that your professors and colleagues mention. If you keep track, too, of questions that occur to you, but that you are unable to pursue immediately, you may find that you are able to do so once you have graduated. If you do not write these down, however, it is unlikely that you will remember them one or two years later.

Recommended readings

Forhan, L. E. and Scheraga, M. (2000). Becoming sociopolitically active. In J. K. Hall and W. Eggington (eds.) *The Sociopolitics of English Language Teaching.* (pp. 195–221) Clevedon: Multilingual Matters.

Bailey, K., Curtis, A., and Nunan, D. (2001). *Pursuing Professional Development: The Self as Source*. Boston, MA: Heinle & Heinle.

Richards, J. C. and Farrell, T. S. C. (2005). *Professional Development for Language Teaching: Strategies for Teacher Learning*. Cambridge: Cambridge University Press.

These three texts provide extensive information and activities that you can engage in for reflective teaching, action research, and professional development.

Egbert, J. (ed.) (2003). *Becoming Contributing Professionals*. Alexandria, VA: TESOL.

Murphey, T. (ed.) (2003). *Extending Professional Contributions*. Alexandria, VA: TESOL.

These two books are the first in TESOL's series of four books on professional development targeted for teachers at different career stages.

Garton, S. and Richards, K. (eds.) (2008). *Professional Encounters in TESOL: Discourses of Teachers in Teaching*. London: Palgrave.

This edited collection provides accounts of ESL teacher development in a variety of international contexts and across the career span, with the first section focused on teachers still in training.

Activities

1. What local and national TESOL-related professional organizations exist in your future teaching location? Look at their website to learn about the kinds of resources, support, and opportunities the association offers.
2. Go to the websites of major publishers of ESL textbooks and teacher education materials and sign up to receive email notices for new books that may be of interest to you. Examples of of these publishers are Cambridge University Press, Heinemann (especially for elementary and secondary ESL materials), Heinle & Heinle, Oxford University Press, Palgrave, Pearson, Routledge, and the University of Michigan Press.
3. Below are two conference proposals and their brief summaries. The first (now published, see Bell, 2009) was submitted as part

of a symposium for AILA's 2005 World Congress. The second was for a paper (see Bell, 2006) which was delivered at AAAL in 2004. Recalling the discussion of genre from Chapter 4, try to identify the parts of each abstract. What similarities and differences do you see and how do you account for them? For example, why do you think the amount of detail regarding methodology is so different between the two proposals?

Abstract 1: Learning about and through humor in the L2 classroom

In order to help language instructors make sense of humor and select appropriate examples to use in their classrooms, several scholars have put forth typologies of humor and made recommendations for the appropriate levels of learners with which each type might be used (e.g., Trachtenberg, 1979; Deneire, 1995; Schmitz, 2002). These propositions are not without controversy. Humorous communication is extremely complex in both its forms and functions (e.g., Norrick, 1993), and much of the previous work has not examined these complexities in the detail necessary for the target audience, classroom language teachers, to be able to make informed judgments concerning the possible role of in their classrooms. In addition, these researchers have not made use of naturally occurring interaction in making their recommendations.

This paper draws on data (interviews, participant observation, and discourse analysis of audio or video taped interaction) collected from three research projects involving the use and understanding of humor by L2 speakers in both classroom and non-classroom situations to illuminate what has so far been a largely theoretical discussion. While Davies (2003) has suggested that the classroom normally cannot provide the type of context necessary for learners to participate in and thus develop competence in L2 humor, I argue that it is appropriate to address L2 humor in the classroom as many learners voice a desire for this and because access to humor is frequently restricted for L2 speakers interacting with NSs outside of educational contexts. I then review recommendations for pedagogical applications of humor in the L2 classroom and use examples to demonstrate how these are inadequate for determining what might be taught and learned and to whom. I close with suggestions for incorporating humor into the language classroom in light of the data presented of learner humor.

Summary 1

While language teachers are advised of the benefits of humor, data of learner humor show how these recommendations inadequately present the complexities of humor, oversimplifying what might be taught and to whom. Humor should, however, be addressed as learners often have little access to it in interaction with NSs.

Abstract 2: Humor in NS–NNS interaction: resources, rights, and representations

The application of sociocultural theory to L2 learning has yielded insights into the ways in which the construction of social identity in interaction can shape L2 proficiency and learners' access to L2 linguistic resources. Joan Kelly Hall (1995) points out that the more social identities are constructed in such a way as to highlight differences, the more (L2) speech will be evaluated *vis-à-vis* the perceived rights of that group membership, rather than viewing the speakers' contributions as those of individuals freely choosing their language. This study demonstrates how, in conversations between NSs and NNSs, humor may act as an especially volatile site for L2 speakers' proficiency and access to linguistic resources to be facilitated or restrained.

This research used case study methodology to document the ways in which L2 verbal humor was negotiated and constructed by three adult female advanced NNSs of English as they interacted with NSs of English. The primary source of data came from tape recordings made over a period of one to two years by the participants of their interaction with NSs. They were also interviewed about their experiences with L2 humor and participated in playback sessions in which their interpretations of portions of the taped interaction were sought. Qualitative and quantitative discourse analysis of these data sources showed how identities were constructed by different participants across different contexts and what the results of these constructions were on the NNSs' L2 use.

In this presentation I focus largely on one participant, showing how her language use varied in contexts in which she was positioned as 'other' to those occasions when she was constructed as a full member of the group. Finally, I compare her situation to that of the other two case study participants and suggest reasons as to why humorous interaction may induce such positioning.

Summary 2

Discourse analysis of conversations between three advanced female L2 users and their NS interlocutors shows how humorous interaction can act as a site in which NNS identities are subject to very different constructions, which in turn affect their proficiency and access to L2 resources.

Conclusion

The main goal of this book has been to prepare you to enter and succeed in an MA TESOL program. We worked toward this in two parts. First, I introduced you to the history and many of the current concepts being examined in the field. We also discussed ways of conceptualizing language, teaching, and learning. In the second part of the text we focused on the actual experience of graduate school and what it might entail, as well as describing ways to position yourself for success on the job market. Throughout the book I have tried to emphasize both the common core of beliefs and concerns shared by ELT professionals, as well as the diversity among these beliefs. If you have used this book as part of a course, this will have become apparent to you as your professor perhaps emphasized points differently, noted areas I have neglected, or disagreed with certain aspects.

Overall, however, I hope that you now feel better equipped to face the challenge of getting your degree and have a better idea of what to expect in the process. I also hope I have conveyed the reality that no MA TESOL program can prepare you for every challenge you will face as a teacher, nor can it cover every topic in depth. Cliché as it may be, being a teacher means being a lifelong learner, and your experiences after graduate school will continue to help you develop as an ELT professional. You should leave your program feeling a part of the TESOL community, sharing in its resources and knowing how to access them.

As I write this Conclusion we are nearing the start of another school year and I find myself regularly engaged in conversations with colleagues where we bemoan our too short break or commiserate about our feelings of unpreparedness. Even many highly experienced teachers will admit to having a few jitters before their first class meetings. We worry about knowing enough and about engaging the students. We look again at the activities that we have planned, checking to see that they are clearly written, and we hope that they lead to better learning outcomes. Then, once courses start, we continue to worry. Our students see us for a few short hours each week, leaving our class to go on to other activities, while we spend the rest of the day filtering much of what we encounter through the lens of that class: 'I could use the scene from this movie as an example for my students!' or 'I wonder if Maya saw the announcement for this guest speaker? It would be a great resource for her project.' Given the all-consuming nature of teaching, sometimes a less demanding job that gets left behind at the end of the day sounds appealing.

Another recent experience helps explain why, despite all this, teaching is something so many people love to do. A friend with whom I had served in the Peace Corps emailed recently with news of a Cameroonian woman who was seeking to contact her former English teachers. Although we had taught her for only a month or so during our training 15 years ago, she remembered all of our names and wished to thank us. All teachers have one or two stories like this one, where students from the past come back to share their appreciation for our work. Far more frequent, however, and even more rewarding are the much smaller triumphs: the joy of watching students becoming so engrossed in an activity that they lose track of time, the satisfaction of having explained something perfectly, the mutual development that comes from teacher–student dialog.

I wish you luck as you start on your new career and welcome you to the profession. I hope this text will serve as a reference as you develop your teaching persona and continue to improve the classroom experience for your students. I would be delighted to hear of your experiences and how this book may have influenced you.

Appendix A
Common Acronyms and Abbreviations in TESOL

ACTFL: American Council on the Teaching of Foreign Languages. The acronym is used for the professional organization and also for the test of L2 proficiency that was developed by that organization.

CALL: computer-assisted language learning

CBI: content-based instruction

CLT: communicative language teaching

EAL: English as an additional language. This term has been used largely in Britain, although its usage may spread, as it avoids the potential confusion of ESL.

EAP: English for Academic Purposes (a subset of ESP)

EFL: English as a foreign language. Traditionally, this refers to English when it is taught or learned in a place where it is not the primary language of communication, such as Japan or Germany.

ELL: English language learner

ELT: English language teaching/training

ESL: English as a second language. This has been used as a contrast to EFL to describe the teaching or learning of English in a place where it is the primary language of communication, such as in Australia or the US. It is also, however, seen as the most general term to describe English language teaching.

ESOL: English to speakers of other languages

ESP: English for specific/special purposes. This refers to, for example, English teaching for engineers or nurses.

FL: foreign language

IELTS: International English Language Testing System

IL: interlanguage

L1: first language

L2: second language. This is often used as a cover term for all additional languages a person knows in addition to their L1, although L3 can be used to specify, for example, the acquisition of a third language.

LEP:	limited/low English proficient/proficiency. The term has been used by K-12 schools in the US, but has fallen into disfavor because of its negative connotations.
NES:	native English speaker
NNES:	non-native English speaker
NNS:	non-native speaker
NS:	native speaker
NL:	native language
SI:	sheltered instruction. This is used mainly in US K-12 schools.
SLA:	second language acquisition
SLL:	second language learning
TBLT:	task-based language teaching
TEFL:	teaching English as a foreign language
TESL:	teaching English as a second language
TESOL:	teachers of English to speakers of other languages (professional organization)
TL:	target language (i.e.; the language that one is attempting to learn)
TOEFL:	Test of English as a Foreign Language
TOEIC:	Test of English for International Communication
TSE:	Test of Spoken English
TWE:	Test of Written English
WE:	World Englishes

Appendix B
Websites for TESOL Information and Professional Development

Applied linguistics associations

http://www.aila.info/ International Association of Applied Linguistics
http://www.aaal.org/ American Association for Applied Linguistics
http://www.baal.org.uk/ British Association for Applied Linguistics
http://www.aclacaal.org/ Canadian Association of Applied Linguistics

TESOL and language education professional associations

http://www.iatefl.org/ International Association of Teachers of English as a
  Foreign Language (find your local affiliate organization here, too)
http://www.tesol.org/ Teachers of English to Speakers of Other Languages
  (find your local affiliate here, too)
http://www.natecla.org.uk/ National Association for Teaching English and
  Other Community Languages to Adults
http://www.tesol.org.au Australian Council of TESOL Associations
http://www.tesl.ca/ TESL Canada

Language education research centers

These usually offer research reports, professional development opportunities,
  and classroom activities based on research.
http://www.cilt.org.uk/ National Centre for Languages
http://www.carla.umn.edu/ Center for Advanced Research on Language
  Acquisition
http://www.cal.org/ Center for Applied Linguistics
http://nflrc.hawaii.edu/ National Foreign Language Resource Center
http://www.ncela.gwu.edu/ National Clearinghouse for English Language
  Acquisition and Language Instruction Educational Programs

Other sources

http://www.conferencealerts.com/ Choose 'linguistics' to see many conferences related to TESOL worldwide
http://www.linguistlist.org/ The Linguist List

Glossary

behaviorism: A psychological approach that saw learning as a process of habit formation, in which the individual responded to some stimulus, received positive or negative reinforcement for their behavior, and either maintained or altered that behavior in the future, based on the feedback. This perspective was popular in the US during the early twentieth century and in applied linguistics is associated in particular with the work of **B. F. Skinner**.

Chomsky, Noam: Linguist best known for his theories of syntax and for proposing the view of language as innate.

communicative competence: This term is used to describe the entire knowledge of language needed to communicate. Rather than simply encompassing grammatical knowledge, it includes rules of how to select and use language appropriately across contexts.

competence: This term refers to a speaker's mental representation or knowledge of language. It is often used in contrast with **performance**, or language use.

Corder, S. Pit: Applied linguist whose contributions include the development of error analysis, the study of interlanguage, and the distinction between error and mistake.

de Saussure, Ferdinand: Early linguist whose works became the basis for what became known as structuralist linguistics.

discourse: In this text 'discourse' refers to language beyond the level of the sentence. From this perspective the study of discourse involves understanding how texts work as cohesive and coherent units. It is important to note, however, that this is a term that is used in distinct ways by different scholars.

English for Specific Purposes (ESP): The term used to describe English instruction that is tailored for the needs of particular groups (e.g., engineers, business people, or airline pilots). English for Academic Purposes (EAP) is considered a subdivision of ESP.

formative assessment: A type of evaluation that is ongoing and serves to facilitate the development of the student. It can be contrasted with **summative assessment**.

form-focused instruction: This term is used to describe instructional techniques that attempt to draw the learner's attention, implicitly or explicitly, to the formal and structural features of the target language within a communicative context.

genre: A genre is a type of text that can be recognized by the typical (or generic) rhetorical features it tends to exhibit with regard to linguistic choices of grammar and vocabulary, as well as content and organization.

Halliday, M. A. K.: Linguist who developed a new approach to linguistics known as Systemic Functional Linguistics. His work has been pivotal in L1 and L2 education, particularly with respect to the notion of **genre**.

Hymes, Dell: Anthropologist whose work with language led SLA scholars to focus on studying the nature and development of **communicative competence**.

informed consent: Refers to the procedure by which participants in a research project are provided with clear and accurate information about the risks and benefits of the study and then are able to decide whether or not they choose to participate. Informed consent is obtained mainly to protect the research participants.

input: This refers to the language to which learners are exposed. This includes both oral and written language.

instrumental motivation: This describes the learning of a language primarily for the purposes of achieving some practical goal, such as gaining university admission or obtaining employment.

integrative motivation: This describe the learning of language primarily with the goal of developing relationships (integrating oneself) with the speakers of that language.

interlanguage: This refers to the L2 learner's still-developing language.

Jakobson, Roman: Prominent structural linguist whose main contributions include linguistic typology and universals.

Krashen, Stephen: Applied linguist who introduced the notion of comprehensible input and developed the Monitor Model, a comprehensive theory of SLA. His work today focuses on literacy and bilingualism.

Lado, Robert: Applied linguist who developed the technique of contrastive analysis used to compare two languages with the goal of developing effective pedagogical approaches.

lingua franca: A language that is commonly used for wider communication in multilingual situations.

modified input: This refers to input that has been adapted to facilitate communication with a non-native speaker. Changes may include shorter sentences, simpler vocabulary, and clearer articulation.

morphology: This is the branch of linguistics that studies the smallest meaningful units of language (morphemes). The word 'cats,' for example, contains two morphemes: *cat* and the plural suffix -*s*.

multicompetence: Vivian Cook introduced this term to describe the state of mind of an individual who knows more than one language.

negative evidence: This refers to language from which the learner can discern what is not grammatical in the target language. Error correction is one type of negative evidence. (See also **positive evidence.**)

negotiation: This describes the interactional and linguistic changes that speakers make in an effort to communicate. It is often referred to more completely as negotiation of meaning.

performance: This term is used to refer to language use, in contrast to language knowledge. (See also **competence.**)

phonetics: Thhe branch of linguistics that seeks to describe the physical properties of language sounds.

phonology: The branch of linguistics that examines the sound inventories of languages and the ways in which these pattern in language. Differences in the sound inventories of languages often result in pronunciation difficulties for L2 learners.

positive evidence: This refers to any input that demonstrates to the learner what is grammatical in the target language. The speech or writing of native speakers generally functions as positive evidence. (See also **negative evidence.**)

postmethod: Braj Kumaravadivelu introduced this term to describe the disciplinary shift from methods provided by experts for teachers, to a more flexible, responsive, and local pedagogy developed by teachers based on sound principles of teaching and learning.

poverty of the stimulus: Thhe name given to Chomsky's assertion that the input received by language learners is of low quality, as it contains disfluent and ungrammatical examples of speech.

pragmatics: The branch of linguistics that examines the ways in which meaning is construed between speakers, and how the context, speakers, and conversational goals influence the ways that this occurs.

recast: A recast is a specific type of feedback, in which the interlocutor reformulates a learner's utterance, correcting any error that occurred.

register: This refers to language varieties used within specific situations. For example, we may use a formal register in giving a speech, or a professional register, such as the language of physicians, in a workplace context.

scaffolding: This refers to developmentally appropriate (that is, neither too much nor too little) support for a learning activity that is provided to a learner by a teacher or more advanced peer and that allows that learner to accomplish the task.

Selinker, Larry: Applied linguist who introduced the term **interlanguage.**

semantics: The branch of linguistics that examines word and sentence meaning.

Skinner, B. F.: Behavioral psychologist whose work contributed to the development of the audiolingual method of language teaching.

summative assessment: This type of evaluation attempts to check on and summarize what a student has learned at a certain point in time. It is contrasted with **formative assessment.**

syntax: The branch of linguistics that studies the rules by which phrases and sentences are constructed.

target language: This refers to the language being learned.

task: In L2 education, a task is an activity that focuses learners' attention on meaning and has a clear goal and outcome. Tasks may also implicitly direct learners' attention to form, but communication is primary.

Vygotsky, Lev: Psychologist whose work on language, thought, and human development has been influential in bringing a view of mental processes as social, as much as cognitive, to applied linguistics.

zone of proximal development: Vygotsky coined this term to describe a metaphorical space between what a learner can do on his or her own and what he or she can achieve with assistance. (See **scaffolding**).

References

Abrams, Z. (2003). The effect of synchronous and asynchronous CMC on oral performance in German. *The Modern Language Journal*, 87(2): 157–67.

Alderson, C. and Banerjee, J. (2001). Language testing and assessment (Part I). *Language Teaching*, 34(4): 213–36.

Alderson, C., and Banerjee, J. (2002). Language testing and assessment (Part II). *Language Teaching*, 35(2): 79–113.

Allwright, D. (1993). Integrating 'research' and 'pedagogy': appropriate criteria and practical possibilities. In J. Edge and K. Richards (eds.) *Teachers Develop Teachers Research* (pp. 125–35). Oxford: Heinemann.

Allwright, D. (2003). Exploratory practice: rethinking practitioner research in language teaching. *Language Teaching Research*, 7(2): 113–41.

Allwright, D. (2005). From teaching points to learning opportunities and beyond. *TESOL Quarterly*, 39(1): 9–32.

Allwright, D. (2006). Six promising directions in applied linguistics. In S. Gieve and I. Miller (eds.) *Understanding the Language Classroom* (pp. 11–17). New York: Palgrave Macmillan.

Allwright, D. and Bailey, K. (1991). *Focus on the language classroom*. Cambridge: Cambridge University Press.

Anton, M. and DiCamilla, F. (1998). Socio-cognitive functions of L1 collaborative interaction in the L2 classroom. *The Canadian Modern Language Review*, 54(3): 314–42.

Auerbach, E. (1993). Reexamining English only in the ESL classroom. *TESOL Quarterly*, 27(1): 9–32.

Auerbach, E. (1995). The politics of the ESL classroom: issues of power in pedagogical choices. In J. Tollefson (ed.) *Power and Inequality in Language Education* (pp. 9–33). Cambridge: Cambridge University Press.

Bachman, L. F. and Palmer, A. S. (1996). *Language Testing in Practice*. Oxford: Oxford University Press.

Bailey, K. (2001). Action research, teacher research, and classroom research in language teaching. In M. Celce-Murcia (ed.) *Teaching English as a Second or Foreign Language*, 3rd edition (pp. 489–98). Boston, MA: Heinle & Heinle.

Bailey, N., Madden, C. and Krashen, S. (1974). Is there a 'natural sequence' in adult second language learning? *Language Learning*, 24(2): 235–43.

Bakhtin, M. (1981). *The Dialogic Imagination*. Austin, TX: University of Texas Press.

Bell, N. (2005). Exploring L2 language play as an aid to SLL: a case study of humour in NS–NNS Interaction. *Applied Linguistics*, 26(2): 192–218.

Bell, N. (2006). Interactional adjustments in humorous intercultural communication. *Intercultural Pragmatics*, 3(1), 1–28.

Bell, N. (2009). Learning about and through humor in the L2 classroom. *Language Teaching Research* 13(3).

Belz, J. (2003). Linguistic perspectives on the development of intercultural competence in telecollaboration. *Language Learning and Technology*, 7(2): 68–117.

Benson, P. (2007). Autonomy in language teaching and learning. *Language Teaching*, 40(1): 21–40.

Beretta, A., Crookes, G., Gregg, K. and Long, M. (1994). Comment on van Lier (1994). *Applied Linguistics*, 15(3): 347.

Bhatia, V. (2004). *Worlds of Written Discourse: A Genre-Based View.* London: Continuum.

Bloch, B. and Trager, G. (1942). *Outline of Linguistic Analysis.* Baltimore, MD: Linguistic Society of America.

Block, D. (1994). A day in the life of an English class: teacher and learner perceptions of task purpose in conflict. *System*, 22(4): 153–75.

Block, D. (1996). Not so fast! Some thoughts on theory culling, relativism, accepted findings and the heart and soul of SLA. *Applied Linguistics*, 17(1): 65–83.

Borg, S. (2003a). Teachers' involvement in TESOL research. *TESOL Matters*, 13(2): 1–8.

Borg, S. (2003b). Teachers, researchers, and research in TESOL: seeking productive relationships. *TESOL Matters*, 13(3).

Bourdieu, P. (1977). The economics of linguistic exchanges. *Social Science Information*, 16(6): 645–68.

Braine, G. (1999). *Nonnative Educators in English Language Teaching.* Mahwah, NJ: Lawrence Erlbaum.

Bremer, K., Roberts, C., Vasseur, M-T., Simonot, M., and Broeder, P. (1996). *Achieving Understanding: Discourse in Intercultural Encounters.* New York: Longman.

Broner, M. and Tarone, E. (2001). Is it fun? Language play in a fifth-grade Spanish immersion classroom. *The Modern Language Journal*, 85(3): 363–79.

Brown, H. D., Tarone, E., Swan, M., Ellis, R., Prodromou, L., Jung, U., Bruton, A., Johnson, K., Nunan, D., Oxford, R. L., Goh, C., Waters, A., and Savignon, S. J. (2006). Forty years of language teaching. *Language Teaching*, 40(2): 1–15.

Brown, R. (1973). *A First Language: The Early Stages.* Cambridge, MA: Harvard University Press.

Brutt-Griffler, J. and Samimy, K. (1999). Revisiting the colonial in the post-colonial: critical praxis for nonnative-English-speaking Teachers in a TESOL program. *TESOL Quarterly*, 33(3): 413–31.

Callahan, R. (2005). Tracking and high school English learners: limiting opportunity to learn. *American Educational Research Journal*, 42(2): 305–28.

Cameron, D., Frazer, E., Harvey, P., Rampton, M. B. H., and Richardson, K. (1992). Introduction. *Researching Language: Issues of Power and Method* (pp. 1–28). London: Routledge.

Canagarajah, S. (1996). From critical research practice to critical research reporting. *TESOL Quarterly*, 30(2): 321–31.

Canagarajah, S. (1999). *Resisting Linguistic Imperialism in English Language Teaching*. Oxford: Oxford University Press.

Canagarajah, S. (2002). *A Geopolitics of Academic Writing*. Pittsburgh, PA: University of Pittsburgh Press.

Canagarajah, S. (2006). Changing communicative needs, revised assessment objectives: testing English as an international language. *Language Assessment Quarterly*, 3(3): 229–42.

Canale, M. and Swain, M. (1980). Theoretical bases of communicative approaches to second language teaching and testing. *Applied Linguistics*, 1(1): 1–47.

Casanave, C. and Vandrick, S. (2003). *Writing for Scholarly Publication: Behind the Scenes in Language Education*. Mahwah, NJ: Lawrence Erlbaum.

Cheng, A. (2008). Analyzing genre exemplars in preparation for writing: the case of an L2 graduate student in the ESP genre-based instructional framework of academic literacy. *Applied Linguistics*, 29(1): 50 71.

Chick, J. K. (1996). Safe talk: collusion in apartheid education. In H. Coleman (ed.) *Society and the Language Classroom* (pp. 21–39). Cambridge: Cambridge University Press.

Chomsky, N. (2002/1957). *Syntactic Structures*, 2nd edition. Berlin: Mouton de Gruyter.

Chomsky, N. (1959). A review of B. F. Skinner's *Verbal Behavior*. *Language*, 35(1): 26–58.

Chomsky, N. (1965). *Aspects of a Theory of Syntax*. Cambridge, MA: MIT Press.

Chun, D. (2008). Computer-mediated discourse in instructed environments. In S. Magnan (ed.) *Mediating Discourse Online* (pp. 15–45). Amsterdam: John Benjamins.

Clarke, M. (2008). *Language Teacher Identities: Co-constructing Discourse and Community*. Clevedon: Multilingual Matters.

Cook, G. (2000). *Language Play, Language Learning*. Oxford: Oxford University Press.

Cook, V. (1991). The poverty-of-the-stimulus argument and multi-competence. *Second Language Research*, 7(2): 103–17.

Cook, V. (1992). Evidence for multi-competence. *Language Learning*, 42(4): 557–91.

Cook, V. (1999). Going beyond the native speaker in language teaching. *TESOL Quarterly*, 33(2): 185–209.

Cortazzi, M. and Jin, L. (1999). Cultural mirrors: materials and methods in the EFL classroom. In E. Hinkel (ed.) *Culture in Second Language Teaching* (pp. 196–219). Cambridge: Cambridge University Press.

Crookes, G. (1993). Action research for second language teachers – going beyond teacher research. *Applied Linguistics*, 14(2): 130–44.

Crystal, D. (2008). Two thousand million? Updates on the statistics of English. *English Today*, 24(1): 3–6.

de Bot K. (2008). Introduction: second language development as a dynamic process. *Modern Language Journal*, 92(2): 166–78.

de Bot, K., Lowie, W., and Verspoor M. (2007). A dynamic systems theory approach to second language acquisition. *Bilingualism: Language and Cognition*, 10(1): 7–21, 51–5.

DeKeyser, R. (1998). Beyond focus on form: cognitive perspectives on learning and practicing second language grammar. In C. Doughty and J. Williams (eds.) *Focus on Form in Classroom Second Language Acquisition* (pp. 42–63). Cambridge: Cambridge University Press.

de Villiers, J. and de Villiers, P. (1973). A cross-sectional study of the development of grammatical morphemes in child speech. *Journal of Psycholinguistic Research*, 2(3): 267–78.

Donato, R. (1994). Collective scaffolding in second language learning. In J. Lantolf and G. Appel (eds.) *Vygotskian Approaches to Second Language Research* (pp. 33–56). Norwood, NJ: Ablex Publishing Company.

Donitsa-Schmidt, S., Inbar, O., and Shohamy, E. (2004). The effects of teaching spoken Arabic on students' attitudes and motivation in Israel. *Modern Language Journal*, 88(2): 217–28.

Dörnyei, Z. (2005). *The Psychology of the Language Learner: Individual Differences in Second Language Acquisition*. New York: Routledge.

Dörnyei, Z. and Csizér, K. (1998). Ten commandments for motivating language learners. *Language Teaching Research*, 2(3): 203–29.

Dörnyei, Z. and Ushioda, E. (eds.) (2009). *Motivation, Language Identity and the L2 Self*. Clevedon: Multilingual Matters.

Doughty, C. and Pica, T. (1986). 'Information gap' tasks: do they facilitate language acquisition? *TESOL Quarterly*, 20(2): 305–25.

Duff, P. and Uchida, Y. (1997). The negotiation of teachers' sociocultural identities and practices in postsecondary EFL classrooms. *TESOL Quarterly*, 31(3): 451–86.

Dulay, H. and Burt, M. (1973). Should we teach children syntax? *Language Learning*, 23(2): 245–58.

Dulay, H. and Burt, M. (1974). Natural sequences in child second language acquisition. *Language Learning*, 24(1): 37–53.

Ellis, N. (1998). Emergentism, connectionism and language learning. *Language Learning*, 48(4): 631–64.

Ellis, N. (2008). The dynamics of second language emergence: cycles of language use, language change, and language acquisition. *Modern Language Journal*, 92(2): 232–49.

Ellis, N. and Larsen-Freeman, D. (2006). Language emergence: implications for applied linguistics – introduction to the special issue. *Applied Linguistics*, 27(4): 558–89.

Ellis, R. (2000). Task-based research and language pedagogy. *Language Teaching Research*, 4(3): 193–220.

Ellis, R. (2003). *Task-based Language Teaching and Learning*. Oxford: Oxford University Press.

Firth, A. and Wagner, J. (1997). On discourse, communication, and (some) fundamental concepts in SLA research. *The Modern Language Journal*, 81(3): 285–300.

Firth, A. and Wagner, J. (1998). SLA property: No trespassing! *The Modern Language Journal*, 82(1): 91–4.

Feez, S. (1998). *Text-Based Syllabus Design*. Sydney: NCELTR, Macquarie University.

Flynn, S. and Lust, B. (2002). A minimalist approach to L2 solves a dilemma of UG. In V. Cook (ed.) *Portraits of the L2 User* (pp. 93–120). Clevedon: Multilingual Matters.

Flynn, S., and Martohardjono, G. (1995). Toward theory-driven language pedagogy. In F. Eckman, D. Highland, P. Lee, J. Milcham, R. Ruthkowski, and R. Weber (eds.) *Second Language Acquisition Theory and Pedagogy* (pp. 45–59). Mahwah, NJ: Lawrence Erlbaum.

Foster, P. and Ohta, A. (2005). Negotiation for meaning and peer assistance in second language classrooms. *Applied Linguistics*, 26(3): 402–30.

Freidson, E. (2001). *Professionalism: The Third Logic*. Chicago: University of Chicago Press.

Frenck-Mestre, C. and Pynte, J. (1997). Syntactic ambiguity resolution while reading in second and native languages. *The Quarterly Journal of Experimental Psychology*, 50A: 119–48.

Gardner, R. and Lambert, W. (1972). *Attitudes and Motivation in Second Language Learning*. Rowley, MA: Newbury House.

Gass, S. (1997). *Input, Interaction, and the Second Language Learner*. Mahwah, NJ: Lawrence Erlbaum.

Gass, S. (1998). Apples and oranges: or why apples are not orange and don't need to be. A response to Firth and Wagner. *The Modern Language Journal*, 82(1): 83–90.

Gass, S. and Mackey, A. (2006). Input, interaction and output: an overview. *AILA Review*, 19, 3–17.

Gass, S. and Makoni, S. (2004). World Applied Linguistics. *AILA Review*, 17.

Gass, S. and Polio, C. (1997). Replication and reporting: a commentary. *Studies in Second Language Acquisition*, 19(4): 499–508.

Gass, S. and Varonis, E. (1985). Variation in native speaker speech modification to non-native speakers. *Studies in Second Language Acquisition*, 7(1): 37–57.

Gee, J. P. (1996). *Social Linguistics and Literacies: Ideology in Discourses*. London: Taylor & Francis.

Gilmore, A. (2007). Authentic materials and authenticity in foreign language learning. *Language Teaching*, 40(2): 97–118.

Graddol, D. (1999). The decline of the native speaker. In D. Graddol and U. H. Meinhof (eds.) *English in a Changing World* (AILA Review 13), 57–68.

Gregg, K. (1984). Krashen's monitor and Occam's razor. *Applied Linguistics*, 5(2): 79–100.

Gregg, K. (1993). Taking explanation seriously; or, Let a couple of flowers bloom. *Applied Linguistics*, 14(3): 276–94.

Gregg, K. (1996). The logical and developmental problems of second language acquisition. In W. Ritchie and T. Bhatia (eds.) *Handbook of Second Language Acquisition* (pp. 49–81). San Diego, CA: Academic Press.

Gregg, K. (2000). A theory for every occasion: postmodernism and SLA. *Second Language Research*, 16(4): 383–99.

Gregg, K., Long, M., Jordan, S., and Beretta A. (1997). Rationality and its discontents in SLA. *Applied Linguistics*, 18(4): 539–59.

Halliday, M. A. K. (1973). *Explorations in the Functions of Language*. New York: Elsevier.

Halliday, M. A. K. (1975). *Learning How to Mean: Explorations in the Development of Language*. London: Edward Arnold.

Halliday, M. A. K. (2004/1969). Relevant models of language. In J. Webster (ed.) *The Language of Early Childhood* (pp. 269–80). London: Continuum.

Harder, P. (1980). Discourse as self-expression: on the reduced personality of the second language learner. *Applied Linguistics*, 1(3), 262–70.

Harklau, L. (2000). From the 'good kids' to the 'worst': representations of English language learners across educational settings. *TESOL Quarterly*, 34(1): 35–67.

Hatch, E. (1978). Discourse analysis and second language acquisition. In E. Hatch (ed.) *Second Language Acquisition: A Book of Readings* (pp. 401–35). Rowley, MA: Newbury House.

Hatch, E. (1983). *Psycholinguistics: A Second Language Perspective*. Rowley, MA: Newbury House.

Heller, M. (1994). *Crosswords: Language, Education and Ethnicity in French Ontario*. New York: Mouton de Gruyter.

Hinkel, E. (1996). When in Rome: evaluations of L2 pragmalinguistic behaviors. *Journal of Pragmatics*, 26, 51–70.

Holliday, A. (2005). *The Struggle to Teach English as an International Language*. Oxford: Oxford University Press.

Hopper, P. (1998). Emergent grammar. In M. Tomasello (ed.) *The New Psychology of Language: Cognitive and Functional Approaches to Language Structure* (pp. 155–76). Mahwah, NJ: Lawrence Erlbaum.

House, J. (1999). Misunderstanding in intercultural communication: interactions in English as a lingua franca and the myth of mutual intelligibility. In C. Gnutzmann (ed.) *Teaching and Learning English as a Global Language* (pp. 73–89). Tübingen: Stauffenburg.

Howatt, A. P. R. with Widdowson, H. G. (2001). *A History of English Language Teaching*. Oxford: Oxford University Press.

Hyland, K. (2004). *Genre and Second Language Writing*. Ann Arbor, MI: University of Michigan Press.

Hymes, D. (1972a). Models of interaction of language and social life. In J. J. Gumperz and D. Hymes (eds.) *Directions in Sociolinguistics: Ethnography of Communication* (pp. 35–71). New York: Holt, Rinehart & Winston.

Hymes, D. (1972b). On communicative competence. In J. B. Pride and J. Holmes (eds.) *Sociolinguistics* (pp. 269–93). Harmondsworth: Penguin Books.

Ibrahim, A. (1999). Becoming black: rap and hip-hop, race, gender, identity, and the politics of ESL learning, *TESOL Quarterly* 33(3): 349–69.

Izumi, Y. and Izumi, S. (2004). Investigating the effects of oral output on the learning of relative clauses in English: issues in the psycholinguistic requirements for effective output tasks. *Canadian Modern Language Review*, 60(5): 587–609.

Jenkins, J. (2000). *The Phonology of English as an International Language: New Models, New Norms, New Goals*. Oxford: Oxford University Press.

Jenkins, J. (2002). A sociolinguistically based empirically researched pronunciation syllabus for English as an international language. *Applied Linguistics*, 23(1): 83–103.

Johns, A. (1995). Teaching classroom and authentic genres: initiating students into academic cultures and discourses. In D. Belcher and G. Braine (eds.) *Academic Writing in a Second Language* (pp. 277–91). Norwood NJ: Ablex.

Johns, A. (2008). Genre awareness for the novice academic student: an ongoing quest. *Language Teaching*, 41(2): 237–52.

Johnston, B. (1997). Do EFL teachers have careers? *TESOL Quarterly*, 31(1): 681–712.

Kachru, B. and Nelson, C. (1996). World Englishes. In S. McKay and N. Hornberger (eds.) *Sociolinguistics in Language Teaching* (pp. 71–102). Cambridge: Cambridge University Press.

Kanno, Y. (2008). *Language and Education in Japan: Unequal Access to Bilingualism*. New York: Palgrave.

Kern, R. (1995). Restructuring classroom interaction with networked computers: effects on quantity and characteristics of language production. *The Modern Language Journal*, 79(4): 457–76.

Kolb, A. (2007). How languages are learnt: primary children's language learning beliefs. *Innovation in Language Learning and Teaching*, 1(2): 227–41.

Kramsch, C. (1993). *Context and Culture in Language Teaching*. Oxford: Oxford University Press.

Kramsch, C. (2002). *Language Acquisition and Language Socialization: Ecological Perspectives*. London: Continuum.

Kramsch, C. and Whiteside, A. (2008). Language ecology in multilingual settings: towards a theory of symbolic competence. *Applied Linguistics*, 29(4): 645–71.

Krashen, S. (1981). *Second Language Acquisition and Second Language Learning*. Oxford: Pergamon.

Krashen, S. (1985). *The Input Hypothesis: Issues and Implications*. London: Longman.

Kubota, R. (2001). Teaching World Englishes to native speakers of English: a pilot project in a high school class. *World Englishes*, 20(1): 47–64.

Kumaravadivelu, B. (1994). The postmethod condition: (e)merging strategies for second/foreign language teaching. *TESOL Quarterly*, 28(1): 27–48.

Kumaravadivelu, B. (2001). Toward a postmethod pedagogy. *TESOL Quarterly*, 35(4): 537–60.

Lado, R. (1957). *Linguistics across Cultures: Applied Linguistics for Language Teachers*. Ann Arbor, MI: University of Michigan Press.

Lantolf, J. (1996). Second language theory building: letting all the flowers bloom! *Language Learning*, 46(4): 713–49.

Lantolf, J. (2000). *Sociocultural Theory and Second Language Learning*. Oxford: Oxford University Press.

Lantolf, J. (2002). Commentary from the Flower Garden: responding to Gregg 2000. *Second Language Research*, 18(1): 113–19.

Lantolf, J. and Poehner, M. (2008). *Sociocultural Theory and the Teaching of Second Languages*. London: Equinox.

Lantolf, J. and Thorne, S. (2006). *Sociocultural Theory and the Genesis of Second Language Development*. Oxford: Oxford University Press.

Larsen-Freeman, D. (1976). An explanation for the morpheme acquisition order of second language learners. *Language Learning*, 26(1): 125–34.

Larsen-Freeman, D. (1997). Chaos/complexity science and second language acquisition. *Applied Linguistics*, 18(2): 141–65.

Larsen-Freeman, D. (2008). Does TESOL share theories with other disciplines? *TESOL Quarterly*, 42(2):291–3.

Larsen-Freeman, D. and Cameron, L. (2008). *Complex Systems and Applied Linguistics*. Oxford: Oxford University Press.

Lea, M. (1994). 'I thought I could write until I came here': student writing in higher education. In D. Graddol and S. Thomas (eds.) *Language in a Changing Europe* (pp. 64–72). Clevedon: BAAL and Multilingual Matters.

Lea, M. and Street, B. (1998). Student writing in higher education: an academic literacies approach. *Studies in Higher Education*, 23(2): 157–72.

Leeman, J. (2003). Recasts and second language development: beyond negative evidence. *Studies in Second Language Acquisition*, 25(1): 37–63.

Lenneberg, E. (1967). *Biological Foundations of Language*. New York: John Wiley & Sons.

Lin, A. M. Y. (1999). Doing-English-lessons in the reproduction or transformation of social worlds? *TESOL Quarterly*, 33(3): 393–412.

Lin, A., Wang, W., Akamatsu, N., and Riazi A. (2002). Appropriating English, expanding identities, and re-visioning the field: from TESOL to teaching English for Glocalized communication (TEGCOM). *Journal of Language, Identity, and Education*, 1(4): 295–316.

Linell, P. (1998). *Approaching Dialogue: Talk, Interaction and Contexts in Dialogical Perspectives*. Amsterdam: John Benjamins.

Lippi-Green, R. (1997). *English with an Accent: Language, Ideology and Discrimination in the United States*. London: Routledge.

Long, M. (1983). Linguistic and conversational adjustments to non-native speakers. *Studies in Second Language Acquisition*, 5(2): 177–93.

Long, M. (1996). The role of the linguistic environment in second language acquisition. In W. Ritchie and T. Bhatia (eds.) *Handbook of Second Language Acquisition* (pp. 413–68). San Diego, CA: Academic Press.

Long, M. (1997). Construct validity in SLA: a response to Firth and Wagner. *The Modern Language Journal*, 81(3): 318–23.

Long, M. (2006). *Problems in SLA*. Mahwah, NJ: Lawrence Erlbaum.

Lyster, R. (1998). Negotiation of form, recasts, and explicit correction in relation to error types and learner repair in immersion classrooms. *Language Learning*, 48(2): 183–218.

Mackey, A. (1999). Input, interaction and second language development. *Studies in Second Language Acquisition*, 21(4): 557–87.

Mackey, A. and Goo, J. (2007). Interaction research in SLA: a meta-analysis and research synthesis. In A. Mackey (ed.) *Conversational Interaction in Second Language Acquisition: A Series of Empirical Studies* (pp. 407–52). Oxford: Oxford University Press.

Martin, J. and Rose, D. (2005). Designing literacy pedagogy: scaffolding democracy in the classroom. In J. Webster, C. Matthiessen, and R. Hasan (eds.) *Continuing Discourse on Language*, vol. 1 (pp. 251–80). London: Continuum.

Martin, J. and Rose, D. (2008). *Genre Relations: Mapping Culture*. London: Equinox.

McKay, S. (2002). *Teaching English as an International Language: Rethinking Goals and Approaches*. Oxford: Oxford University Press.

McKay, S. and Wong, S. C. (1996). Multiple discourses, multiple identities: investment and agency in second language learning among Chinese adolescent immigrant students. *Harvard Educational Review*, 66(3): 577–608.

McLaughlin, B. (1987). *Theories of Second Language Learning*. London: Edward Arnold.

McNamara, T. (2008). Mapping the scope of theory in TESOL. *TESOL Quarterly*, 42(2): 302–4.

McNamara, T. (2004). Language testing. In A. Davies and C. Elder (eds.) *The Handbook of Applied Linguistics* (pp. 763–83). Malden, MA: Blackwell.

Medgyes, P. (1992). Native or non-native: who's worth more? *ELT Journal*, 46(4): 340–9.

Miller, J. (2004). Identity and language use: the politics of speaking ESL in schools. In A. Pavlenko and A. Blackledge (eds.) *Negotiation of Identities in Multilingual Contexts* (pp. 290–315). Clevedon: Multilingual Matters.

Mitchell, C. and Vidal, K. (2001). Weighing the ways of the flow: twentieth-century language instruction. *Modern Language Journal*, 85(1): 26–38.

Morgan-Short, K. and Wood, H. B. (2006). Processing instruction and meaningful output-based instruction: effects on second language development. *Studies in Second Language Acquisition*, 28(1): 31–65.

Moussu, L. and Llurda, E. (2008). Non-native English-speaking English language teachers: history and research. *Language Teaching Research*, 41(3): 315–48.

Musumeci, D. (1997). *Breaking Tradition: An Exploration of the Historical Relationship between Theory and Practice in Second Language Teaching*. Boston, MA: McGraw-Hill.

Nassaji, H. and Wells, G. (2000). What's the use of 'triadic dialogue'? An investigation of teacher–student interaction. *Applied Linguistics*, 21(3): 376–406.

Nayar, P. (1997). ESL/EFL dichotomy today: language politics or pragmatics? *TESOL Quarterly*, 31(1): 9–37.

Nicholas, H., Lightbown, P., and Spada, N. (2001). Recasts as feedback to language learners. *Language Learning*, 54(4): 719–58.

Norris, J. and Ortega, L. (2000). Effectiveness of L2 instruction: a research synthesis and quantitative meta-analysis. *Language Learning*, 50(3): 417–528.

Norton, B. (2000). *Identity and Language Learning: Gender, Ethnicity and Educational Change.* Harlow: Longman/Pearson Education.

Norton Peirce, B. (1995). Social identity, investment, and language learning. *TESOL Quarterly,* 29(1): 9–31.

Nunan, D. (1993). Action research in language education. In J. Edge and K. Richards (eds.) *Teachers Develop Teachers Research* (pp. 39–50). Oxford: Heinemann.

Nunan, D. (1995). Closing the gap between learning and instruction. *TESOL Quarterly,* 29(1): 133–58.

Ogbu, J. (1983). Minority status and schooling in plural societies. *Comparative Education Review,* 27(2): 168–90.

O'Grady, W. (2008). The emergentist program. *Lingua,* 118: 447–64.

Obler, L. (1989). Exceptional language learners. In S. Gass, C. Madden, D. Preston, and L. Selinker (eds.) *Variation in Second Language Acquisition.* Volume II: *Psycholinguistic Issues* (pp. 141–59). Clevedon: Multilingual Matters.

Ohta, A. (1995). Applying sociocultural theory to an analysis of learner discourse: learner–learner collaborative interaction in the zone of proximal development. *Issues in Applied Linguistics,* 6(2): 93–121.

Oxford, R. (1990). *Language Learning Strategies: What Every Teacher Should Know.* Boston: Heinle & Heinle.

Painter, C. (1999). *Learning through Language in Early Childhood.* London: Cassell.

Paltridge, B. (2001). *Genre and the Language Learning Classroom.* Ann Arbor, MI: University of Michigan Press.

Pavlenko, A. (2003). 'I never knew I was a bilingual': reimagining teacher identities in TESOL. *Journal of Language, Identity and Education,* 2(4): 251–68.

Pavlenko, A. and Lantolf, J. (2000). Second language learning as participation and the (re)construction of selves. In J. Lantolf (ed.) *Sociocultural Theory and Second Language Learning* (pp. 155–77). Oxford: Oxford University Press.

Pennycook, A. (1996). Borrowing others' words: text, ownership, memory, and plagiarism. *TESOL Quarterly,* 30(2): 201–30.

Pennycook, A. (2003). Global Englishes, Rip Slyme, and performativity. *Journal of Sociolinguistics,* 7(4): 513–33.

Pennycook, A. (2004). Performativity and language studies. *Critical Inquiry in Language Studies,* 1(1): 1–19.

Phillipson, R. (1992). *Linguistic Imperialism.* Oxford: Oxford University Press.

Philp, J. (2003). Constraints on noticing the gap: nonnative speakers' noticing of recasts in NS–NNS interaction. *Studies in Second Language Acquisition,* 25(1): 99–126.

Pica, T. (1994). Research on negotiation: what does it reveal about second language learning conditions, processes, and outcomes? *Language Learning,* 44(3): 493–527.

Pica, T., Lincoln-Porter, F., Paninos, D., and Linnell, J. (1996). Language learners' interaction: how does it address the input, output, and feedback needs of L2 learners? *TESOL Quarterly,* 30(1): 59–84.

Pomerantz, A. and Bell, N. (2007). Learning to play, playing to learn: FL learners as multicompetent language users. *Applied Linguistics*, 28(4): 566–78.

Ramanathan, V., Davies, C. E., and Schleppegrell, M. (2001). A naturalistic inquiry into the cultures of two divergent MA-TESOL programs: implications for TESOL. *TESOL Quarterly*, 35(2): 279–305.

Rampton, B. (1990). Displacing the 'native speaker': expertise, affiliation, and inheritance. *ELT Journal*, 44(2): 97–101.

Reagan, T. (2004). Objectification, positivism and language studies: a reconsideration. *Critical Inquiry in Language Studies*, 1(1): 41–60.

Richards, J. C. and Lockhart, C. (1996). *Reflective Teaching in Second Language Classrooms*. Cambridge: Cambridge University Press.

Richards, J.C. and Rodgers, T. S. (2001). *Approaches and Methods in Language Teaching*. Cambridge: Cambridge University Press.

Richards, K. (2006). 'Being the teacher': identity and classroom conversation. *Applied Linguistics*, 27(1): 51–77.

Riggenbach, H. (1999). *Discourse Analysis in the Language Classroom*. Ann Arbor, MI: University of Michigan Press.

Sapir, E. (1921). *Language: An Introduction to the Study of Speech*. New York: Harcourt Brace. Also available online at http://www.bartleby.com/186/.

Schmenk, B. (2005). Globalizing learner autonomy. *TESOL Quarterly*, 39(1): 107–18.

Schön, D. (1983). *The Reflective Practitioner*. New York: Basic Books.

Seidlhofer, B. (1999). Double standards: teacher education in the expanding circle. *World Englishes*, 18(2): 233–45.

Seidlhofer, B. (2004). Research perspectives on teaching English as a lingua franca. *Annual Review of Applied Linguistics*, 24: 209–39.

Sfard, A. (1998). On two metaphors for learning and the dangers of choosing just one. *Educational Researcher*, 27(2): 4–13.

Sharwood Smith, M. (1981). Consciousness-raising and the second language learner. *Applied Linguistics*, 2(2): 159–68.

Shea, D. (1994). Perspective and production: structuring conversational participation across cultural borders. *Pragmatics*, 4(3): 357–89.

Shohamy, E. (2005). The power of tests over teachers: the power of teachers over tests. In D. Tedick (ed.) *Second Language Teacher Education: International Perspectives* (pp. 101–11). Mahwah, NJ: Lawrence Erlbaum Associates.

Siegal, M. (1996). The role of learner subjectivity in second language sociolinguistic competency: Western women learning Japanese. *Applied Linguistics*, 17(3): 356–82.

Sinclair, J. M. and Coulthard, M. (1975). *Towards an Analysis of Discourse*. Oxford: Oxford University Press.

Singleton, D. (2005). The Critical Period Hypothesis: a coat of many colours. *IRAL*, 43: 269–85.

Skinner, B. F. (1957). *Verbal Behavior*. New York: Appleton-Century-Crofts.

Slimani, A. (1992) Evaluation of classroom interaction. In J. C. Alderson and A. Beretta (eds.) *Evaluating Second Language Education* (pp. 197–211). Cambridge: Cambridge University Press.

Spada, N. and Lightbown, P. (2008). Form-focused instruction: isolated or integrated? *TESOL Quarterly*, 42(2): 181–207.

Stewart, T. (2006). Teacher–researcher collaboration or teachers' research? *TESOL Quarterly*, 40(2): 421–30.

Svalberg, A. (2007). Language awareness and language learning. *Language Teaching*, 40(4): 287–308.

Swain, M. (1985). Communicative competence: some roles of comprehensible input and comprehensible output in its development. In S. Gass and C. Madden (eds.) *Input in Second Language Acquisition* (pp. 235–53). Rowley, MA: Newbury House.

Swain, M. (2000). The output hypothesis and beyond: mediating acquisition through collaborative dialogue. In J. Lantolf (ed.) *Sociocultural Theory and Second Language Learning* (pp. 97–114). Oxford: Oxford University Press.

Swain, M. (2006). Languaging, agency and collaboration in advanced second language learning. In H. Byrnes (ed.) *Advanced Language Learning: The Contributions of Halliday and Vygotsky* (pp. 95–108). London: Continuum.

Swain, M. and Lapkin, S. (2000). Task-based second language learning: the uses of the first language. *Language Teaching Research*, 4(3): 251–74.

Swain, M. and Lapkin, S. (2002). Talking it through: two French immersion learners' response to reformulation. *International Journal of Educational Research*, 37(3/4): 285–304.

Swain, M. and Lapkin, S. (2006). 'Oh, I get it now!' From production to comprehension in second language learning. In D. M. Brinton and O. Kagan (eds.) *Heritage Language Acquisition: A New Field Emerging* (pp. 301–20). Mahwah, NJ: Lawrence Erlbaum.

Swales, J. (1990). *Genre Analysis: English in Academic and Research Settings*. Cambridge: Cambridge University Press.

Tarone, E. (2006). Language lessons: a complex, local co-production of all participants. In S. Gieve and I. Miller (eds.) *Understanding the Language Classroom* (pp. 163–74). New York: Palgrave Macmillan.

Thomas, J. (1983). Cross-cultural pragmatic failure. *Applied Linguistics*, 4(2): 91–112.

Tocalli-Beller, A., and Swain, M. (2007). Riddles and puns in the ESL classroom: adults talk to learn. In A. Mackey (ed.) *Conversational Interaction in Second Language Acquisition: Empirical Studies* (pp. 143–67). Oxford: Oxford University Press.

Tokowicz, N. and MacWhinney, B. (2005). Implicit and explicit measures of sensitivity to violations in second language grammar: an event-related potential investigation. *Studies in Second Language Acquisition*, 27(2): 173–204.

Tomlinson, B. (1998). *Materials Development in Language Teaching*. Cambridge: Cambridge University Press.

Tomlinson, B. (2003). *Developing Materials for Language Teaching*. London: Continuum.

Tsui, A. B. M. (2003). *Understanding Expertise in Teaching: Case Studies of ESL Teachers*. Cambridge: Cambridge University Press.

Turnbull, M. and Arnett, K. (2002). Teachers' uses of the target and first languages in second and foreign language classrooms. *Annual Review of Applied Linguistics*, 22: 204–18.

Turner, E. and Bitchener, J. (2006). Literature reviews and the concept of argument: evaluating an EAL teaching approach. *New Zealand Studies in Applied Linguistics*, 12(2): 17–36.

van den Branden, K. (2006). *Task-Based Language Education: From Theory to Practice*. Cambridge: Cambridge University Press.

van Lier, L. (1994). Forks and hope: pursuing understanding in different ways. *Applied Linguistics*, 15(3): 328–47.

van Lier, L. (2004). *The Ecology and Semiotics of Language Learning: A Sociocultural Perspective*. Boston, MA: Kluwer Academic Publishers.

van Lier, L. (2007). Action-based teaching, autonomy, and identity. *Innovation in Language Teaching and Learning*, 1(1): 46–65.

VanPatten, B. and Williams, J. (2007). *Theories in Second Language Acquisition: An Introduction*. Mahwah, NJ: Lawrence Erlbaum.

Vygotsky, L. S. (1978). *Mind in Society: The Development of Higher Psychological Processes*. Cambridge, MA: Harvard University Press.

Wajnryb, R. (1990). *Grammar Dictation*. Oxford: Oxford University Press.

Waring, H. (2008). Using explicit positive assessment in the language classroom: IRF, feedback, and learning opportunities. *The Modern Language Journal*, 92: 577–94.

White, L. (1989). *Universal Grammar and Second Language Acquisition*. Amsterdam: John Benjamins.

White, L. (2003). *Second Language Acquisition and Universal Grammar*. Cambridge: Cambridge University Press.

Widdowson, H. G. (1994). The ownership of English. *TESOL Quarterly*, 28(2): 377–89.

Widdowson, H. G. (2003). *Defining Issues in English Language Teaching*. Oxford: Oxford University Press.

Wolfson, N., D'Amico-Reisner, L., and Huber, L. (1983). How to arrange for social commitments in American English: the invitation. In N. Wolfson and E. Judd (eds.) *Sociolinguistics and Language Acquisition* (pp. 116–28). Rowley, MA: Newbury House.

Index